Praise for *Everything Good ab*

"There's a lot of bad music out there. But [...] mean we should give up on all music. There's a lot of bad religion out there, but that doesn't mean we should reject all faith and spirituality. This book is a reminder that the answer to bad theology isn't no theology; it is good theology. We need to reclaim our faith from the folks who have used it to camouflage their bigotry. We need to live out a version of Christianity that is beautiful and loving and worth believing in. In this manifesto of love, my friend Bruce Reyes-Chow invites us all to acknowledge the damage that has been done in the name of Christ, but he also dares us to refuse to let the bad news be the only news. He challenges us to reclaim our faith. Thank God that Jesus has survived the embarrassing things Christians have done in his name. Read this book, and let's live out a version of our faith that is music to the ears of God and a precious melody in the ears of all those longing to love and be loved."

—**Shane Claiborne**, author, activist, and
cofounder of Red Letter Christians

"For a generation that continually finds ourselves questioning and re-questioning the very idea of religious 'truth,' Bruce Reyes-Chow has delivered a gift of a book right on time, promising us that we can still find comfort in the Divine One we've long loved—not in spite of Mystery, but because of it."

—**Shannon K. Evans**, author of *Feminist Prayers
for My Daughter* and *Rewilding Motherhood*

"Now and then, a nudging yet persistent voice reminds us that the ways we live out our faith commitments require both attention and reconsideration. With this book, Bruce Reyes-Chow becomes that voice, giving us not only new language to communicate traditional themes on the church's theological register, but an applied framework that allows those themes to become germane to one's faith imperatives and passions. From the first lines you will feel addressed by that voice, and I am convinced you will find the quality of its sound to be clear, honest, winsome, sharp, and defiantly hopeful."

—**José R. Irizarry**, president and professor of practical theology, Austin Presbyterian Theological Seminary

"Bruce Reyes-Chow's book refuses to concede Christianity to extremism and makes the compelling case for a Christian practice that is rooted in openness, reconciliation, justice, truth, and love. As a pastor, biblical scholar, and anti-poverty activist, I have always been taken that the 'faith of Jesus' and 'faith in Jesus' are written the same in biblical Greek. This book shows how faith in a justice-seeking, inclusive, all-loving God holds true to the faith that Jesus embodies."

—**Rev. Dr. Liz Theoharis**, director, Kairos Center, and co-chair, Poor People's Campaign: A National Call for Moral Revival

"When it comes to faith and spirituality, some people feel like they're on the outside trying to get in, and others feel like they're on the inside looking for a way out. Both groups will love Bruce Reyes-Chow's new book. He names the parts of religion that so many of us are trying to get away from, and he introduces an understanding of faith in God that so many of us would like to be part of. Highly recommended!"

—**Brian D. McLaren**, author of *Faith After Doubt*

"Bruce Reyes-Chow articulates what so many of us are quietly thinking: that there are valuable goods in this Christian story worth carrying forward. When our faith is hijacked, the solution is not to turn over the keys; it's to say and live what we know to be true. *Everything Good about God Is True* offers a much-needed catechesis—one of liberation and love and justice—that gives voice to our longings for a God beyond both our construction and our deconstruction. This is a must-read for all who sense that something in this faith is worth salvaging."

—**Grace Ji-Sun Kim**, Professor of Theology at Earlham School of Religion, and author of *Invisible*, *Spirit Life*, and *Reimagining Spirit*

"Bruce Reyes-Chow invites the reader to sit down for a chat. In a conversational style, he asks questions about the Christian faith and responds with examples and understandings of his own life. But it doesn't stop there: the reader is asked to engage and respond through their own understandings and experiences. He strips away the baggage of what we 'must' or 'ought to' believe so that the reader can begin to articulate their own experience of God, Jesus, and the Holy Spirit and how this informs community and right relationships. Reyes-Chow provides a way for us to explore authentic relationships with God, others, and self."

—**Karen P. Oliveto**, United Methodist bishop, and author of *Together at the Table* and *Our Strangely Warmed Hearts*

Everything Good about God Is True

BRUCE REYES-CHOW

Everything Good about God Is True

CHOOSING FAITH

Broadleaf Books
Minneapolis

EVERYTHING GOOD ABOUT GOD IS TRUE
Choosing Faith

Library of Congress Control Number 2023947867 (print)

Cover design: Stephanie Sumulong

Print ISBN: 978-1-5064-9569-9
eBook ISBN: 978-1-5064-9570-5

To ancestors, saints, and generations past;
communities, compadres, and collaborators of today;
and activists, academics, artists, and adventurers yet to come

Contents

Introduction

At the end of 2021, the world lost a giant in the struggle for human dignity and the fight for social justice. I had just started writing this book when Archbishop Desmond Tutu died, and his death reminded me of my one interaction with the presence, wisdom, and joy that was Desmond Tutu.

In 2009 I had the privilege of attending the inauguration of the 44th president of the United States of America, Barack Hussein Obama. During inauguration week, I took in the inauguration festivities around the DC, attended the official inauguration worship service held at the National Cathedral, and froze on the National Mall with thousands of others as we witnessed the inauguration of the first Black president of the United States. The highlight of the week was participating in the processional of the Congressional Black Caucus inauguration worship service, which took place as part of the inauguration festivities. As the then-moderator of the Presbyterian Church (USA)—the highest elected office in a denomination of, at that point, over two million people—I was invited to represent the PC(USA) in the long line of denominational and political dignitaries.

These formalities came with the position in which I found myself, and I was doing my best to fit in. As a very nonfancy, middle-aged dad of three, I felt much more comfortable spending the day tending to my houseplant jungle, on the soccer sidelines cheering on my kids, or lounging on the couch watching reruns of *The Fresh Prince*. Here, in this group of religious movers and shakers, I was definitely out of my element. So of course, as the Spirit or fate or luck would have it, when we lined up, I found myself standing right behind the former archbishop of Cape Town.

Desmond Tutu was the focus of the entire room full of people. I could feel the eyes of everyone upon him and, in their peripheral vision, on me. I can only imagine what these other leaders were thinking. "Who's that youngish, not tall Asian American dude—and how the heck did he get to stand next to Bishop Tutu?" If I were them, I would have given me the side-eye too. But I tried to focus. I mean, how often do you get to stand next to an icon of the anti-apartheid movement?

So there I stood as we waited to process to the front, for what seemed like a lifetime. Now, I can chat it up with most people, and I'm rarely at a loss for words, but I was dying to talk to him and I had nothing. What was I going to lead with? "So Bishop, how was your flight?" "Whatcha been bingeing on Netflix these days?" "This Barack thing: pretty crazy, right?" This was DESMOND TUTU, for God's sake. There simply *was* no worthy opening line.

Yet as his grace would have it, before I said something that would bring shame upon my family, my ancestors, and my denomination, he started chatting with me . . . like a regular person.

Of course he did! He asked me about myself, my family, and the church I served. He engaged me with all the exuberance and joy he was known for. During one of the most significant events in US history, this larger-than-life human saw me. This holy man, who had played a significant role in the dismantling of South Africa's system of apartheid, been imprisoned for his efforts, and worked to bring healing to his nation, asked me about my kids, my job, and my ordinary little life.

Right then, right there, he saw me when he sure didn't have to. He could have turned to any number of more powerful people, for we were surrounded by them. But his power and influence came from his humble acknowledgment of our collective humanity and love for us all. And while Bishop Tutu was not God, through his honest and genuine gesture, God was made known to me.

That night the bishop preached a gleeful, prophetic sermon, moving his seventy-year-old body like a teenager as he danced with the gospel hip-hop duo Mary Mary. The night ended with the sanctuary filled with political, religious, and cultural leaders, most of them African American, singing the Black national anthem, "Lift Every Voice." The groans of generations mingled with the exuberant shouts claiming a new day, hope for tomorrow, and pure joy.

At the center was a man who had grown up under apartheid, led a nonviolent movement that resulted in the overthrow of a regime that had dedicated itself to racist oppression, and modeled a courageous, faithful, and genuine version of faith. His Christian faith challenged his country to be the kind of place that he believed God intended, one of equality, justice, and humanity.

This much is clear: We who identify as Christian or Christian-ish in the United States—insiders to the church and outsiders, "believers" and doubters, Protestants and Catholics, evangelicals and mainliners—need a different story of Christianity than the one that is dominating right now. We need a gospel that looks more like the faith that animated Bishop Tutu before he died: compassionately just, beautifully complex, and excruciatingly kind.

I fear that here in the United States we are losing our collective imagination for the common good. We have barricaded ourselves behind false boundaries of wealth, security, and privilege. We have broken apart any common understanding of what it means to be the body politic and what it means to pursue liberty and justice for everyone.

And Christians have been at the center of it all.

Is everything bad about Christianity true?

If you are reading this book in the 2050s, I hope you all have your clean-energy-powered jet packs and that pumpkin-spice anything has finally been designated as an affront to culinary decency. I also hope that the world has made a ginormous political and social course correction. Right now, in the 2020s, words like *surreal, unprecedented,* and *unbelievable* fail miserably to convey the cataclysmic dumpster fire in which we have found ourselves. I wish words like *dystopian* and *apocalyptic* were hyperbolic. Looking back, the past few years have proved that few acts, political or personal, are off the table.

If you did not have the pleasure of living through these times, pop on your time-traveling virtual-reality goggles and set your destination date to January 6, 2021. We find ourselves just after the 2020 election, and the Capitol building and Congress are being attacked by a group of white nationalist insurrectionists, supported by public officials, who are determined to disrupt the peaceful transition of power and the official certification of president-elect Joe Biden. Death chants can be heard echoing through the halls, names are being called out, nooses are being waved toward the Capitol, and people are being beaten with barricades and flag poles. We are on the brink of a political coup, and we will soon learn exactly how thin a thread our democracy is hanging on. Most sickening and enraging is the fact that, in the days and months to follow, not all political parties will condemn it.

Around this same time, the economic gaps between those who hold a disproportionate amount of wealth and those shackled by poverty are widening at an alarming rate, limiting access to education, healthcare, and the basic survival needs of millions of people. Reproductive rights in some states are reverting to the 1920s, with some states criminalizing abortion and forcing humans to give birth no matter the situation or circumstance. Gun violence and mass shootings are everyday events, even as state officials increase open-carry laws, call on educators to arm themselves, and exert no political will to address this health crisis. Boards of education across the country are creating false narratives around racism, sexuality, and gender that are leading to book bannings and the criminalization of teaching about the history or the realities of race, sexuality, and gender. Every week we hear of another instance of police brutality leading to the death of Black and brown people, but there is no substantial movement to fundamentally change public safety practices; in fact, the funding and militarization of local law enforcement systems are increasing.

Meanwhile, self-appointed militias, vigilante mobs, and white nationalist hate groups posing as patriots and protectors are taking it upon themselves to harass, intimidate, and threaten violence toward immigrants, asylum seekers, and refugees at our borders; drag queens reading stories at libraries; folks marching in support of human rights, racial justice, or reproductive rights; as well as anyone who affirms or identifies as part of LGBTQIA+ communities. Basically anyone who does not wear the political garments of a white evangelical Christian nationalist "American" is fair game—and yes, "game" as in huntable, shootable, and killable.

Welcome to the 2020s.

Sadly, this is not an exhaustive list. I wish it were. But hate never ceases to surprise. Every day humans find ways to exclude, oppress, and otherwise create more division, not less.

Yes, there are many who have not been part of the white evangelical Christian nationalist movements. But whether we like it or not, *that* is the dominant Christian narrative of the day. Voices that claim to be about "religious freedom" are, in reality, pushing for a theocratic country and expressing a nationalism dominated by a culture of white, straight, male, conservative, evangelical, fundamentalist Christianity. This brand of Christianity's decades-long political effort is meant to legislate certain ideas of what society should look like, what activities should be allowed, and which humans deserve to be treated with dignity—and which do not.

Make no mistake: these voices move us ever closer to a society with legalized religious inquisition and unapologetic spiritual apartheid. What might have sounded like fear-mongering hyperbole a few years ago—predictions of a civil war in the United States—no longer seems that crazy.

Sometimes it seems like everything bad about Christianity just might be true.

How can we be sure there's a better version?

We are in trouble, no doubt. No wonder those of us within or adjacent to Christianity sometimes want to run the other way. Better to be quiet, fade into the background, abdicate our positions of power and influence, or simply pretend we have nothing to do with *that* version of the faith. No wonder so many have deconstructed their way out of the faith entirely.

But those of us who make any claim to Christianity must not distance ourselves from what is happening. So much of what had been taking place was founded upon, reinforced by, and enacted by those who come from a Christian perspective, one that we need to roundly and loudly repudiate and reject. It is incumbent upon Christians in the United States who believe that our faith has been hijacked to offer something better. It is urgent. Christian nationalists profess a gospel of exclusion that limits the expansive possibility of God's creativity. It's a faith built upon a theological absolutism that causes us to know God less, not more.

I am writing this book, which repudiates that version of Christianity by offering a better one, because I believe deeply that these are not simply abstract theological, ideological, or political debates. This warped kind of faith leads to death: death of the body, death of relationships, death of faith. LGBTQIA+ folks are driven to death by suicide and death by violence inflicted by others; immigrants end up dying in the middle of deserts trying to seek bodily safety and economic opportunity; the environment is hemorrhaging; Black and brown people are being killed and incarcerated into chronic invisibility; and the unjust distribution of wealth and resources keeps people in poverty, unhoused, and starving. The list goes on. These examples are not hyperbolic, slippery-slope rhetorical examples. They are realities that we know to be true. And they are what drive many of us to fight theologies that are taking society further down this path of hate-filled division and destruction.

All this leads to why I am making an audacious and somewhat arrogant claim: That there is a better version of the gospel of Jesus Christ. That Christianity can actually be a healing balm for a hurt and hurting world. That there is, simply, a *better* choice of Christian faith.

Isn't that kind of arrogant? you may say. How dare you claim that what you believe is better than anyone else? Isn't that what you accuse *them* of doing?

All are appropriate questions. But the reality is we *all* believe there are better—and therefore worse—ways to do things. Parenting, cooking, sports, and yes, faith: we all believe that some ways of doing these things are better than others. I do not claim that I offer the One True Faith or the Only Way. But I firmly believe there is a more complex, nuanced, loving, and just version of the gospel that is bubbling just beneath the surface of our social consciousness, ready for widespread renewal and rediscovery. These pages contain almost everything I believe about God, complete with all the joyful wandering, misdirected confidence, and revelatory doubt that brings life to my faith.

The Christian story that I present in this book, and the one I believe Jesus embodies and Scripture contains, invites—nay, *requires*—a struggle with belief. This gospel also challenges us to live out those beliefs in the world as if we actually believed them to be true. There is a better way, one that leads with love, empathy, and kindness, and one that leads to liberation, healing, and new life. It's the one that the Samaritan woman invited her friends to encounter when she told them, after having met Jesus at a well, "Come and see the one who has told me everything I've done! Could this one be the Christ?" (John 4:29).

Unlike many of my friends, who were steeped in toxic Christianity and have since tried to get as far away from it as possible, I have called this faith my home for many years. Each year I become a little more grateful that those versions of the Christian story did not inform the faith passed down to me (props to Trinity Presbyterian Church in Stockton, California!). While no gathering of humans is perfect, Trinity, my childhood church, is where I witnessed and received unconditional love, support, and sustenance during times of crisis and struggle. That community of faith taught me to explore, embrace, and celebrate the complexities of life, love, and faith. Trinity taught me the impact of community organizing and activism through our connection to the local school and city politics. Trinity taught me the importance of remembering my ancestors and reminded me to be present for generations to come. What I offer to you on these pages is a version of the Christian faith that has been received, cultivated, practiced, and adapted by a generation who then passed it down to the next and equipped them to do the same. I submit to you that what has been passed to me, and what I hope to pass on to others, is worth retaining.

Please note that the title of this book is *Everything Good about God Is True* and not *Everything People Say about God Is Good*. I fully admit that "good" is a relative term and that the title may sound arrogant and brash. What one person perceives as good may not be experienced as good by another. Yet goodness exists outside our human definition of it—both mine and yours—and in these pages I am inviting you to be a theologian: someone who explores the nature of God in the world and makes claims about what is indeed good about God. We will all struggle with who God is and how God interacts with us, and we will all spend our lives trying to define the "good." I invite you to explore beliefs about God and expressions of faith that I not only believe are *good* but are timelessly *true*.

In this book, I don't offer you a gospel bound up in and defined by regulation, rigidity, and litmus tests. Rather, I attempt to provide an accessible primer on the Christian faith that offers up a vision of faith characterized by acceptance, curiosity, creativity, liberation, love, and what it *is* more than what it is *not*. I strive to offer accessible and clear explanations of significant theological concepts: about God, the Spirit, Jesus, and the church, as well as Christian involvement in public policy and the body politic. I hope this book can offer the "what's next" for people who are deconstructing—all in two hundred pages or less!

So yes, this book rebukes versions of Christianity that are claiming so much space in the national conversation. But make no mistake: We must do more than rebuke and reject and repudiate. We must boldly and unapologetically proclaim and choose a different way. We must choose a more loving, healing, and just way of following Jesus.

Now, before some pastor somewhere writes the first scathing review of this book from their big-ass oak desk that includes "There is nothing new here" or "But he left so much out!"—they will get no disagreement from me. In many ways, this book is simply a culmination of decades of ancestors and saints of the faith shaping my relationship with God. My contribution is unique only insofar as I also encourage you to boldly share a version of the gospel that has nurtured so many of us so well and for so long.

We can no longer abdicate the Christian story to hate, violence, and oppression. Those of us who occupy this more loving, just, and extended version of the Christian story must do a better job of claiming, articulating, and speaking the hell up.

But how do I learn the language?

During the summer of 2021 and after two-plus years of pandemic life, I agreed to take *Minecraft* lessons from my five-year-old nephew. For those of you with no gamers in your life, *Minecraft* is an online game where you build cities, fight things, and do other stuff . . . I think. We didn't get very far in our lesson before discovering that I did not have the tools, language, or instincts for this. As an expertise- and skill-building session, it was an utter failure. My nephew assumed too much about what I already knew about gaming and used words I'd never heard to tell me what to do. "Just create a world" meant nothing to me when I had no idea what a world was in the sanctuary of *Minecraft*. In the end, my nephew had to basically control my avatar's movement, build a world, and join worlds he had already created. However, as a nephew–uncle relationship marker, it was a wild success. Despite my failure to master the world of *Minecraft*, we now have that "Remember that time you tried to teach me *Minecraft*?" memory.

As someone who spent more than a decade leading a new church in San Francisco, I constantly needed to translate churchy words and practices for those who genuinely had no church experience, positive or negative. The experience I had with my nephew mirrors how many folks experience the church when they are exploring the possibility of faith. Most churches are competent at presenting the general gist of what things are, how things happen, and even whispers of what they believe. But when it comes to the nitty-gritty, church people like me tend to make far too many assumptions, most notably that faith is passed down through osmosis, obligation, and potlucks. We assume that what we believe is clear, that people understand all the words, and that what we do makes sense. We think that communicating "belief" is unnecessary, condescending, and below us.

We come by these approaches honestly. Yet we end up giving the impression that we don't really have any foundational beliefs at all, or at least any that we're willing to share. Sure, we may be generally welcoming, but ultimately folks are left on the outside looking in—not for lack of desire on their part but simply because we, the churchy ones, have forgotten how to articulate our faith. We've forgotten that there's a vocabulary of faith that can guide, accompany, usher—pick your metaphor—all of us into a deeper, more nuanced Christian faith. We've forgotten how the expansiveness of God, the journey of Jesus Christ, and the proddings of the Spirit can be lived out in the world, how so many actions of love and liberation are deeply grounded in and reinforced by faith like Desmond Tutu's.

When you think of Christianity, you might identify less with my nephew in the story—the insider, the teacher, the One Who Knows—and more with me. You may be the one interested in learning about this thing called faith but unable to grasp the vocabulary because no one has figured out how to explain or model or teach it. You may feel baffled, inept, and totally out of your element. I write as an insider of this world, so I run the risk of creating and reinforcing spaces of confusion, exclusion, and insider-ese. The Christian faith is more than a video game, and the last thing that I want to do is for you to identify with my newbie gamer experience when it comes to exploring this faith. Apologies for when I fail in this endeavor.

Maybe you are reading this book because someone in church has given it to you. Maybe you've had a bad church experience and yearn for a reminder of what you *used* to believe as good. Or maybe you've had a great experience in church and you're simply trying to get another view, another version of the gospel to think about, or to refresh yourself, or to have as a book study.

No matter where we find ourselves, I believe faith requires daily choices. I believe faith happens in that space between mediocre, inspired, and excruciating. I am here for a faith that has the power to change myself and the world but is also about every day: where I experience the divine in the everyday rhythms of life, see the power in the nuance of human interaction, and find beauty in the creation that surrounds us. Faith judged by measurable progress, human accolades, and religious accomplishment is false faith, and I choose each and every morning not to have any of it. I hope you will not either.

This book is my audacious claim that Christianity does not have to be bound by the trappings of productivity, guilt, competition, shame, or purity culture. I am not laying out a case to convince you to believe in the goodness and presence of God or the power and holiness of the one we know as Jesus Christ. Trying to prove—in mere words—why someone should believe: that's a fool's errand. The pages that follow are a glimpse into a faith that has formed me and one that has been passed along to me from earlier generations. Sure, it's a faith that gets shaped by culture and context. But at the end of the day, it's a durable, lasting story of faith, one that I sincerely believe can bring healing to the world.

Some traditions are built upon the idea that security and belonging are best known through rigidly defined steps and a calcified set of beliefs: doctrines that will guarantee some reward at the end of life. Any questions—about belief or institution or scripture—are seen as signs of weakness and a lack of faith. But I believe belonging is found in the exact opposite: in understanding that context dictates how we move the world, and in letting our beliefs shift. I believe we find true security and belonging by rejecting any transactional endeavors in which we attempt to earn God's love. What if we viewed questions and curiosity as vital elements of a strong, secure faith? What if this approach to faith is not theological relativism but an expansive approach to faith that takes the movements of the Spirit and ever-revealing truths of God seriously? What if, by choosing faith, we learn to ask better questions?

If you are hoping for a direct map from point A to point B, this will be a disappointing book. The story is intentionally winding and wandering, because I choose to believe that it is precisely in the exploration where we best grow to know the divine in ourselves and in the world.

Are you a theologian?

Speaking of God: As the title indicates, this book claps back to the warped version of a God who emboldens hate, supports oppression, rejoices in suffering, and reinforces marginalization. It maintains that all the good things that so many of us have understood to be true are, in fact, *true*: that God is accepting of difference, expansive in perspective, loving of all creation, righteous in the face of injustice, compassionate in times of sorrow, and kind—always kind. No matter what you've heard about God in the past, no matter what you are hearing said about God today, I want to say that all these good things that you have imagined God to be are, in fact, true. Yes, life will cause us to doubt, waver, and reject. But each day we can choose, again and again, to believe that everything good about God is indeed true.

No, I cannot provide empirical evidence that what I have just said about God is true. Rather, I choose to believe in the words and ways that God has spoken to me through the communities that have raised me, the strangers who have surprised me, the loved ones who have loved me, and the many moments of wrestling with the Spirit, conversing with God, reading Scripture, and observing the world.

Many books about faith are written by people with kickass experiences: dramatic and life-altering events that have forced the writer toward monumental transformation. This book is not those. In fact, this is where I come swooping into view with the less-than-inspiring grandeur of some random brown sparrow that you barely even notice at the bird feeder because, well, we're flippin' everywhere. I bring no compelling origin story other than what I have and continue to find holiness and meaning in every day. Sure, I have had my share of drama and struggle, but haven't we all? What I have to offer is a story of choosing faith: not because life forced me to make a choice, but because life has made itself clear that there are a series of choices to be made every day, every hour, every moment. And it is precisely in the cracks and crevices of these moments where I still meet the divine that my faith comes alive, and I choose this journey with Christ over and over again.

I am as surprised as anyone else that I am writing this book about faith and theology. I believe, on one level, that we are all theologians, but for most of my life, I have resisted embracing the idea that *I* am one. Descriptors like "public theologian" can seem so pretentious. Plus, I did not want to disrespect my friends and colleagues who are legit academic theologians who sacrificed so much to get those PhDs. For many people, their image of theologians is a bunch of old white dudes with British accents sitting in a room droning on about patripassianism, latifundalization, or syncretism. First, *yawn*, and second, I *did* pay some attention in seminary. Thankfully, in many places, the realities and persons in those rooms are changing. There are many Black, brown, young, queer, female-identifying, and otherwise diverse theologians out there speaking into theological conversations.

But, like it or not, doing this work of faith is theological work. I am not an academic, but together you and I can expand what it means to be theologians. Together, as theologians, we can wrestle with our relationship to God. As theologians, we can listen for and translate the movement of the Spirit with our communities. Should we choose to acknowledge it, we theologians are holding in tension bold and courageous claims, all the while leaving room for the proddings of our heart, mind, and gut for the guidance of the divine. This theologian thing is quite the adventure. So all together now, doing our best "I am Spartacus!" impression, no matter where you are— café, church pew, the dentist's chair, or waiting in line at the grocery store—say to yourself, "I am a theologian!"

I promise no answers, I offer no destination, and I am not trying to convince anyone of anything (if you are questioning why you bought this book, then *fair enough*). What I do offer is a view of the full landscape of the faith that I am determined to practice every day. I hope that, in doing so, it will help as you practice yours. I hope that, by reading some stories of how I have encountered God, you will take your own stories more seriously. This is a faith of embraced mediocrity, excruciating discernment, joyful liberation, and unexpected revelation. Our everyday experiences are portals through which we encounter God. If everything good about God is indeed true, we learn that goodness each time we take a breath and each day we get to be alive.

What is a faith montage?

I am suspicious whenever I hear truisms like "Everyone should have a mission statement for their life." It's as if all we need to succeed is some catchy little saying cross-stitched on a pillow. I cringe whenever I hear a self-help guru give off a sound-bite motivational parrot vibe (yes, I have issues).

That said, there is something appealing to me about the discipline of claiming what you believe. For as much as I hate trite personal mission statements, and even though our beliefs shift and expand over time, we all have core beliefs. We all express our values, whether or not there is a framed poster of a majestic mountain scene at the golden hour with the word "BLESSED" plastered across it. So, with a dash of chagrin, a little bit of cringe, and a heaped scoop of humility, this is where I begin: with a mission statement. In this case, it is a statement of belief crafted and molded into what I call a faith montage.

Montages are a series of brief moments spliced together to create a whole. They're a bunch of short clips strung together to create an impression, a summary, a feeling. A good montage succinctly and effectively communicates place, personality, growth, breadth, and movement. The mid-film montage is a rom-com movie staple. The scene usually consists of someone trying on outfits in front of their friends or a couple falling in love while wandering the streets of New York, Paris, or an old-timey farm. Montages help the story progress without wasting precious production minutes.

The chapters in this book are built around my own faith montage, which serves as a framework for this sweeping primer on the Christian faith. Each chapter contains snippets of my faith montage. You'll find my full faith montage, as well as guidance for creating your own, in the back of the book. I hope this is a compelling invitation for you to ponder your own list or poem or statement of things you choose to believe about God.

My faith montage is a story, a prayer, a poem, a catechism. Okay, fine, it's a personal mission statement. (Darn you, motivational spiritual gurus!) This prayer will feel comfortable and lovingly worn for some of you, while for others it will be like hearing a foreign tongue (much like my nephew's gaming instructions sounded to me). Hopefully it will hold just enough familiarity for you not to feel completely lost.

I also know that some words will likely, for many of you, trigger pain and trauma from past hurts perpetrated by those supposedly acting in the name of God. Your past interactions with toxic Christian spaces may have left you battered, bruised, and disillusioned with faith. For this, I am deeply sorry. While I will not presume to apologize on behalf of other church leaders, please know that you are not alone. I hope that if you still feel pangs of hurt when talking about faith, you will feel loved and seen in these pages. Even reading this book is an act of courage, so I hope to honor the choice you have made to do so.

I try to stay away from church jargon and Christian-ese as best I can, but I have no illusions that any amount of creative prose will make it feel any less dense. I hope to give texture and depth to words that may have lost their luster or meaning but are worth holding onto in order to find a common language with others on this path of faith. My faith montage is intentionally packed with ideas and concepts, and I do not apologize for the complex and winding nature of this prayer. Our relationship with God is often complex, sometimes contradictory, and constantly evolving. My theological positions have changed and evolved over time, and I expect that they will continue to do so until I take my final breath.

Whether you read my full faith montage at the back of the book all at once or read it as it is revealed chapter by chapter, I hope that you will return to it as you craft your own, whether by writing, drawing, sculpting, or another approach. Read it as a meandering prayer that draws you in new directions and not as a direct map that lands you in a particular place. After you read it once, reread it, this time as a familiar self-guided tour of faith, and see where it takes you. My faith montage is meant to be a progression of beliefs, a library of ideas, and an invitation to theological exploration. Pick and choose where you start and stop. Notice words and phrases that speak to you. Note the places where you feel discomfort because of past experiences or instinctual resistance. Notice the moments of unexpected exhale, brought on by familiar or new ideas. Reflect on how particular phrases land with you. From one line to the next, be open to the affirmation of what you already believe to be true and surprised by something new that stirs your soul.

And through it all, I hope you will also be critical in noticing what is missing, what questions are not addressed, and what is perhaps being avoided. In many ways, any faith montage acts as a kind of "Frequently Asked Questions" for faith, an invitation to further exploration and inquiry. Trust your instincts and curiosity to dive deeper when you feel so moved. I hope you feel all the feels, experience some glimpses of common faith, and try on the title of "theologian." I hope you unapologetically and unabashedly explore your relationship with and understanding of God.

The end of each chapter includes a few questions that may prompt more individual and communal inquiry about faith, a challenge to begin to craft your own faith montage, and a breathing prayer. A breathing prayer (often called a breath prayer) is a simple prayer that you can repeat throughout your day, inhaling as you pray one phrase and exhaling as you pray another.

Should you choose to craft your own faith montage, it will be about who you are in and amid a relationship with God. You will deconstruct long-held beliefs, shed systems that no longer serve your journey and, hopefully, build a theological, spiritual, and holy space. That space may not remain the same for the rest of your life, but it can be a potent and powerful expression of who you are now and who you understand God to be.

Okay, let's do this.

One

A Few Words about the Creator and Us

My oldest child got kicked out of preschool.

The story begins one day on a playground in San Francisco. My wife and I are not big people, so apparently we make small humans. Ev, our eldest, was the first of our three small children, so whenever some kid organized a recess rendition of "family" on the playground, Ev was always cast as the baby.

One day another child, whom we shall call Z., decided to make sure that my baby human understood their place in the recess family. Over and over and over again Z. would proclaim, "Evelyn is a baby!" "Evelyn, you're a baby." "You're so small, you are a baby." "Baby, baby, baby!" "We should pick Evelyn up because Ev is the BABY!"

At a certain point, Ev decided to take matters into their own hands, literally. They picked up the closest stick and smacked Z. across the head.

Stop applauding.

I mean it: stop applauding.

So of course I get a call from the principal, who said, "Mr. Reyes-Chow. When you come in to pick up Evelyn today, could you please stop by my office?"

Being the courageous man-child I am, and after a few moments of hive-inducing flashbacks of being called to the principal's office as a youngster, I called my wife, Robin. "Hey, Hon, would you mind picking Evelyn up today from preschool?"

Robin rejected my plea, so off I skulked to the Principal C.'s office to get my kid. Ms. C. wore a crisp black suit, her makeup was done just so, and she gave serious sophisticated and put-together vibes. I am sure that she was not scary in real life, but first-grade Bruce, who was now showing up in her office, found her absolutely terrifying.

After sitting down, Ms. C. began the story and told me what had happened. Honestly, I'm sitting there, thinking, "Well, Z. deserved it." But as per my parental duty, I took Ev outside and gave them a talking to. This is how the conversation went.

> *Me*: "So Ev, did anything happen today on the playground?"
> *Ev*: "Yeah, Z. got hit with a stick."
> *Me*: "Um, okay. Anything else?" *Ev was not lying.*
> *Ev*: "I had to sit on the bench." *Again, not lying. But oh boy, we were in trouble as parents.*
> *Me*, barely able to keep a straight face: "Were those two things connected at all?"

To their credit, Ev now filled me in on the story and told me how angry they had gotten. We talked about anger and what to do with it. Eventually I asked them, "Ev, why do you think you did it?"

Ev looked me in the eye and said, with total sincerity, "Dad, that's just the way God made me."

Holey moley, this child had been listening! We as parents, and the communities of faith around them, had been telling Ev, during the entirety of their little life, that they were indeed created by God. They, like all humans, were beautifully and wonderfully made.

So we begin where Ev did: by knowing and choosing to believe in the promises of a God who offered us a covenant: "This is the sign of the covenant I am making between me and you and every living creature with you, a covenant for all generations to come: I have set my rainbow in the clouds, and it will be the sign of the covenant between me and the earth" (Genesis 9:12–13).

You will notice that I do not explicitly use the Trinity to describe God. The Trinity is not explicitly mentioned in the Bible, and, rather than try to make sense of the Trinity as a concept, I have chosen to spend more time on the three elements of the overarching entity that we know as God: Creator, Christ, and Holy Spirit. Just as people can hold a multitude of expressions, so can God. God is all three and more, all three and more are God. Over the next few chapters, I offer you some core beliefs about God: what it means for us to believe in God, what it means for people to be gathered around God, and how God shows up, in the breadth and depth of human experience, to those who choose to respond to this calling to be church. I center these first few chapters on our relationship with God as the grand and generous gatherer of humanity. Knowing the impossibility of proving the existence of God, I hope to make God real by describing how the true power of the Creator God exists in the rhythms of life, with us.

First, a few words about what it means to choose to believe in God. Here is the first line of my faith montage.

What does it mean to choose faith in God?

I choose to believe that, in life and in death, I belong to God.

I believe that God is good. Choosing to believe this simple truth compels me to move through the world in a certain way.

Someone told me the other day that science appears, more and more, to be proving the existence of God. In some scientific circles, there is a growing sense that an ultimate being created the universe. In all honesty, I am not sure exactly what science they were referring to or where they were getting their information from, but they were confident that scientists will soon be able to prove the existence of God.

That's all well and good, and I'm happy to hear it. But personally, I don't need science to prove to me that God exists. God is not a hypothesis to prove or a theory to test. Believing in God—that God has created us, guides us, cares for us, and nurtures us—is a choice. It's an act of faith, and one that defies human imagination, rationality, and yes, even science.

I don't even wish to incontrovertibly convince people of the existence of God. I don't want to argue that it makes sense to believe in God, because making this choice is an act of faith. Believing in God is a choice to believe in something bigger than the confines of our own imaginations. In some ways, requiring an empirical underpinning of faith takes away the very beauty, power, and mystery of our relationship with God. I worry that basing belief on empirical evidence can render faith nothing more than another transactional, hollow act—one that attempts to solve the world's need for the very beauty, power, and mystery that God offers.

What I *can* tell you with confidence is that "in life and death" means just that: In the goodness of life, we belong to God, and in the despair of life, we belong to God. In the exploration of life, we belong to God and in the suffering of life: yes, we belong to God. This does not mean that God *causes* all of those things or makes Godself known in the same way in each moment—only that as we venture through these times, we can know that God is with us through it all.

For me and for many others, the belief in God simply happens, unexpectedly, at a certain time, or slowly, through a collection of moments, or simply as a gift. At a certain time, you just believe that there is a God: a powerful Force, an expansive Creator, a mysterious Presence. No matter how you choose to describe God, we can choose to believe that it is God who gives our life direction. We are not on our own navigating the world. At the end of the day, through God and with God, we are more than we could be without God.

Does choosing to believe in God change how I live?

God stirs my soul.
In the morning, life-giving first breath fills my lungs.
God stills my spirit.
In the evening, the calm of the night flows through my body.
God moves me.
The Holy One beckons me forth, through bands of light,
into coves of darkness, woven into rainbows, and amid the
in-between and unknown—

It's actually quite inconvenient to believe in God. We can't simply live life picking and choosing when and how we want to acknowledge God. Some people can compartmentalize when and if they will listen to God. But for me, choosing to live in faith means that every day—every morning, afternoon, and evening—I commit to a life worthy of this God in whom we have chosen to believe. It really does not matter if the world is radiating beauty and kindness over all creation, or if the traumas and tragedies of the day are becoming too weighty to hold, or if the chaotic whiplash of hope and despair makes me to want to crawl into a hole and hide: I will only make it through those times with integrity and self-respect if I remember that God is there through it all.

Many Christians act differently in church than they do in the rest of their lives—and not in a good way. To only claim God when it is convenient is an exercise in compartmentalizing our morals and ethics. Choosing to believe in the goodness of God means living a life of faith and integrity.

I wish I could say that if you choose to believe in God, all good things will happen to you. I wish I could say that if you choose to believe in God, the pain and despair in your life and the lives of loved ones around you will disappear. I wish I could say that if you choose to believe in God, all your doubts, questions, and confusions would be answered and that the suffering, violence, and destruction in the world would make sense.

As much as I would love to be able to say these things, they would be lies, because choosing to believe in God is not a transactional decision. Choosing to believe in God is not a promise of ease, comfort, security, or station. In fact, it often leads to difficult choices, because sometimes believing in the presence of God every day means not knowing where God may be leading us tomorrow.

If I believe in God, does God believe in me?

All the while, with every tender breath,
I am reminded of God's hoping, yearning, and dreaming
that I grow into all I am intended to become.

Choosing to remember and believe in God also means trusting that God remembers and believes in us. It's comforting to know that a powerful Presence is always keeping us in mind. Even when we forget about God—for hours or days or months or even years—God isn't forgetting us.

During the worst moments of life, I find great comfort and guidance in knowing that God has hopes for each of us. Each day God the Creator has intentions for each of us, greater than we could imagine for ourselves. Choosing to believe this compels me to seek out God's guidance.

God's constant presence and repeated healing are comforting. Knowing that God believes in me and in who I can become is one of the main reasons that I choose over and over again to believe in God. If you believe in a God who believes in you, you can walk through the most difficult times knowing that God is with you.

REFLECT

Individual: What have you been taught about God in the past?

Communal: What has community taught you about God?

Practical: Can you remember a time when the presence of God was made known to you?

Montage: What are three beliefs that you have about the nature of God?

BREATHE

Inhale: "God, are you there?"

Exhale: "God, I am open to you."

Two

Grounded

Twenty years ago I almost died. When I first arrived at the emer-
gency room, it was overcrowded, and I found myself on a gurney
in the hallway, literally trying to climb the walls because I was in so
much pain. The doctors had not yet diagnosed my problem, so there
was no pain management plan.

Eventually I learned that I was having a bout of pancreatitis, and
the doctors explained that my angry pancreas was basically digesting
me from the inside out. For a month, I weathered a pain that never
seemed to subside. The doctors tried everything, tested for everything, and still they could not get rid of the pain. I'd weep uncontrol-
lably as another wave of pain engulfed my body, and I would ask God
over and over again, "Why?" and "When will it end?" I was mentally,
emotionally, and spiritually stripped down, bare, and raw. Perhaps
you've been there too.

That pain is hard to explain in words, but so, too, are the
moments in which I felt something else. Somehow, in the middle of
that immense suffering—despite how much I questioned or cursed
God—I experienced a grounding, a solace. Brief respites from the
pain and increasing moments of healing brought a sense that God

could receive all that I had to offer with generosity, tenderness, and care.

Even when we want to give up, we are still held by and surrounded by the presence of God.

What is God's presence?

I am GROUNDED in the presence of God.
God knows me.
God sees me.
God loves me.
And that is enough.

God is with me.
God has been with me.
God will always be with me.

There's no better feeling than knowing that you are seen, known, held, loved, respected, and understood for being exactly who you are—that you are enough. In a world that tells us that we should all be driven by more, more, more, no matter what we are going through, knowing that we are enough for God can keep us grounded and hopeful.

Some versions of Christianity attempt to define exactly what is enough, as if there is a cause-and-effect relationship between what we say and do and how much God loves or is present with us. "God will love you more if you pray more!" "God loves you more because you have more." "God will love you more if you give more." "God loves you more because you have achieved more." It's almost as if God's "enough" can be quantified in the same way that we can check the balance of a bank account or assess the completion of tasks.

But God's "enough" runs way beyond that, reminding us that in our being—including all of the ways that we mess up—we are enough. This does not mean that we are no longer responsible for our actions. It simply means that God gives us the courage to do better the next time, to grow as humans, and to reject the accumulation of material wealth or human accolades.

How and where is God known and present with us?

Through crawling minutes and blurred decades,
mundane whispers and shouts of magnificence,
awkward encounters and an impassioned embrace,
brisk breezes, warm skies, cool fog, living deserts, flourishing
forests, living water,
the farm, the field, the town, the suburb, the streets, and the city,
during protests, parties, feasts, and funerals,
at coffee shops, clubs, stages, pitches, courts, corners, classrooms,
playgrounds, porches,
barbershops, dining tables, couches, screens, and every unexpected
holy space

I'll get to some more specifics later in this book, but what is important to know right now is that God is always with us. And no, I don't mean that God is some creepy, lurking, anthropomorphized entity who is always surveilling us—remember, God is good. Rather, God is accessible and present, always, and wherever we are.

Part of choosing to believe in God and living as if this belief matters is knowing that God is simply present all the time. God is present in the daily rhythms of my life, not only during the good and grand times. God is there in the quiet weeping and the silent wonder. I take comfort that God is present through the ebbs and flows and the valleys and the peaks. Choose your metaphor for the ups and downs of life, but know that God is present in the midst of it all.

Sometimes when people say "God is everywhere" they actually mean "God is most places." But I actually mean *everywhere*. I believe God is present in the wideness of the sky as well as the specifics of our lives: where we call home, outside in creation, on city sidewalks, in a darkened performance space, and in line at school pick-up. Wherever you and I may travel and wherever we may gather, we can know that God, too, is there. We don't need to organize our life in some specific way so that God shows up. We don't need to create the ambience or curate some kind of stage worthy of God being present. God is already here.

Let me be very clear: God does not only show up in church. God does not show up only in places that claim to worship God in a particular way, in a particular setting, or with a particular style. God is present whether you are in a church that has candles and a mighty organ, or a building that is falling apart because you just haven't had the resources to fix it, or a building that is brand new, or a gymnasium, a kitchen, or a park: wherever you may gather as the church, know that God is there. The church can give us ways to connect with God. The church gathers God's people in different ways. But make no mistake: God doesn't need the church to be present with us, and we don't need a church building to know God.

Why is it important to remember that God is always with us?

Through and in it all, God is known to my soul,
and I am reminded that I am known by God.

Sometimes life is terrible, humans are terrible, and the world is terrible. We either choose to believe that the terribleness of the world will have the last word, or we choose to believe that the goodness of God will. When we choose faith, we choose to believe that ultimately, eventually, the goodness of God prevails.

I am deeply familiar with the question that plagues so many: that is, if God is so great, then why do all these terrible things happen? My response is that the question itself gives validity to the idea of a puppeteer God: a God who controls everyone and everything like pieces on a chess board. That version of God is transactional: a God who is about retribution and reward rather than a God of presence.

The goodness of the Creator exists in the midst of and alongside so much pain in the world and in our lives that it would be easy to forget that God is with us through it all. But if we forget the possibilities of God, we give the last word to the stagnation and struggle of the world. God is present through it all, hoping that as we navigate the world, we can be better today than we were yesterday and better tomorrow than we are today. When we think we are alone, struggling with pain or conflict, or when we are doing acts of healing, justice, and compassion, God is present, cheering and championing us to keep moving, keep exploring, and keep growing.

When we remember God, in many ways we remember ourselves. Remembering God grounds us. Yet even when we don't remember God, God remembers us.

REFLECT

Individual: How has God reminded you that you are known and seen by God?

Communal: Through what communities have you most experienced God?

Practical: Is there a setting where you are most attuned to God's presence?

Montage: What are a few ways that you believe God shows up to you?

BREATHE

Inhale: "God is here."
Exhale: "I am here."

Three

Gathered

My mother is one of the most hospitable people I know. Growing up, I'd often come home, whether to a random midweek dinner or a holiday celebration, and there'd be at least one or two people I didn't know at the table. My mom had a knack for inviting people into our lives and into our community in a way that I hope I have passed down to my children.

If my mom invited you over, you weren't a guest or on display as the poor rescued orphan. When you sat at our table, you were immediately part of the family. On your first visit, we'd get you something to drink and feed you. After that, we'd show you where things were in the kitchen and then you were on your own, just like the rest of us. And I tell you: Our family bought into the survival-of-the-fittest meal plan big time. If you didn't get your food, get your drink, and grab your chair, somebody else might get it first. When you accepted that invitation to join us, you became part of the family.

A passage of Scripture that has always moved me is Luke 13:34, when Jesus tells his disciples, "How often have I desired to gather your children together as a hen gathers her brood under her wings." I hold out hope that when God's people gather, we are bit like the crew that would pull up chairs at my mother's table: inviting, genuine, and always loving. In the gathering, we experience healing and comfort. In the gathering, we find belonging and community. In the gathering, we know safety and nourishment.

What's so special about people gathering around God?

Created in the image of God,
I choose to join with others as God's GATHERED.

At some point in many church services, you will hear something like this: "God has brought us here, to this particular place, at this particular time, for a particular reason." This phrase contains one of the holiest and most healing aspects of God for me, because it reminds me that, no matter the magnificence or minutiae of the moment, God has gathered this particular grouping of people for a particular purpose for this moment in time. Whenever I attend or lead a service of worship, I invariably look around at the congregation at some point and think: How on earth did this particular group of people end up together? In these times of such social division, it really is an amazing thing to behold.

Of course, many churches still uphold and practice blatantly exclusionary practices. Yet many churches are also places of deep and true belonging. And at any given gathering, I am moved by this striking realization: there is no other place that this particular grouping of people would be in the same room together. The common draw is not the PTA, a youth sport, a shared hobby, or a political rally. Rather, this group of people have felt some inexplicable calling to gather together to discover a little more about our faith and our relationship to God in the world.

Gathering with Christians does not guarantee anything about who we become. It will not give us a perfect experience of God, nor a perfect experience of humanity. Church is simply a place where we learn and grow and stretch and act and move and do all the things that people do together to grow into who God hopes us to be. Gathering as a body, the body of Christ, brings other perspectives into my worldview and mine into other's. This act is a simple and yet powerful acknowledgment that together we each have the potential to grow and thrive more than we would on our own.

What's so special about people who gather in God?

We are the body gathered,
beautiful, powerful, holy bodies.
These bodies are of all shapes, sizes, abilities, and hues.
These bodies move through the world
    loving and loved,
    desiring and desired,
    healing and healed.

These bodies hold tightly and tenderly the complexities of being:
attractions, peeves, passions, scars, successes, traumas, triggers,
desires, rejections, revelry, heartbreak, intentions, rage, rapture,
miscues, magnificence, contradictions, courage, determination,
discombobulation, dwelling, doubt.

Beautiful and complicated creatures seeking and being sought,
committed and compelled humans navigating the complexities of
the world,
and people loved beyond our imagination by the One who beckons
us forth.

The church at its best—and I say this in the most affectionate way possible—is a place for misfits. It's a place for those who don't belong anywhere else, where belonging is not based on appearance or abilities or fiscal situations. It's not a place of conformity or homogeneity. What makes you a little different? What makes you a little prickly? What quirk gives you character? Ideally, church lets us all bring our full selves. There are very few places where such a group of misfits could gather.

In church we gather around this irrational belief that Someone in the universe is calling us to be different—and not just different alone, but different *together*. Someone has called us into the space and invited us to be fully who we are, with our pains and our sorrows, our hopes and our glee. Unlike anywhere else in the world, we can bring our full selves into this space.

Is there one best, true pathway to God?

By dirt roads and oceans vast, across concrete highways and infinite skies
by coercion and by consequence, by circumstance, and by choice—
our journeys converge.

Some of you reading this book have been deeply hurt by the church. You may have been taught a faith driven by fear, guilt, and shame. You may have been taught a faith that preached blatant and subtle exclusion: racism, misogyny, queerphobia, Islamophobia, xenophobia. And you may have been taught that the only way that you or anyone could ever truly know God was through confession that Jesus was your Lord and Savior. (Spoiler alert: I will argue later that Christianity is *a* way to connect to God and not *the only* way to connect to God.)

To be abundantly clear, I and many others reject and repudiate this version of the gospel. The theological stream I just described and that we looked at in the first chapter is more about justifying the perpetuation of power and domination and less about seeking love and liberation. If you are moving out of this kind of space, I grieve your experience, and I commend you for being open to the possibility that there is another way—a more loving, humble, just, and nuanced way—to believe in God.

Or perhaps your faith has become stale, disconnected, or calcified. Maybe you have been living your faith by osmosis, passed down and borrowed from generations before. Some of you likely grew up without any religious or spiritual presence. Your parents or guardians or caregivers allowed you to search out faith entirely on your own, and so now you are doing just that.

No matter how you are finding your way toward God: Know that this pastor encourages your exploration and curiosity. Seek out your own path with the Creator. There is no one right way to do this, so don't let anybody tell you that the only way that you can truly be a believer is to claim a particular doctrine. Of course we can do certain spiritual disciplines and religious practices to stretch and change and expand our understanding of who God is. But those are not prerequisites for having a deep relationship with God.

How is God-centered community distinctive?

Ancestors and saints,
  generations past,
  generations of today,
  and generations yet to come.

We arrive, we mingle, and we observe.
We step forward, we step back, we pause, we try again.
We engage in a divine dance,
   these bodies, the body
   all in a space that is God's

Church people like to complain about meetings. We say this or that meeting was not run well, the decisions weren't right, or the people were just annoying. It's like we've never gone to a meeting of the PTA or the union or the school board!

I actually think churches do meetings pretty well. While church folks in meetings may disagree about who God is, we can agree that God is our motivation. We believe that God has intentions—hopes and dreams for the world and for us—and that it's our job to figure out who God wants us to be. The fact that our understandings of God are so diverse can make our decision-making confusing, but I think it also makes it more whole. Unlike a business meeting, in which we gather to make a profit, legitimize expenditures, and measure success, church meetings are different—or at least they should be. Unlike a political gathering, in which we engage politics and value partisanship, church meetings say: God is present. And while we don't always do it in the best way, we generally understand that God wants us to be kinder and gentler with one another than we want to be.

Also, when humans gather, we can be super awkward. Church gatherings are no different. When a bunch of humans try to figure out what it means to faithfully gather as the people of God, it's bound to get awkward. But when church people are at our best, we give one another the benefit of the doubt and some slack when it comes to social graces. Because God is the gatherer, we open ourselves to the possibilities of encountering God as we encounter each other.

We can take comfort in knowing that our ancestors have passed the gift of community down to us. We don't have to make this all up on our own or feel pressure to discover every new thing. God isn't just about us here, right now, this particular group of misfits. God is about the work of humanity, from generation to generation. God reminds us that, beyond the world's imagination and even our own, we are gathered together in a particular place, at a particular time, for a particular reason.

Are God's gatherings always positive?

These bodies embody the depth and texture of the Divine,
   seen and unseen,
   known and unknown,
   addressed and avoided.

These bodies are not always in control,
   minds betraying,
   bodies breaking down,
   emotions in disarray,
   mind, body, and spirit,
   swirling, swirling, swirling.

Misfits and strangers uniquely gathered like no place other.
   Gathered by love,
   gathered to love,
   gathered even when we are unable to love,
   and gathered especially when we feel undeserving of love.

I am not anti-happiness, but I *am* anti-toxic positivity: the facade that pretends that everything is always okay. This posture seems to communicate, "If we don't name the pain, then the pain is not really there." This is simply not healthy or healing. There is pain, suffering, and struggle, and we must acknowledge them.

The main purpose of gatherings of Christians is not to give people a false sense of happiness, but to speak into people's lives the complexities and possibilities of hope. Genuine, faithful gatherings invite us to bring our entire selves, both the beauty and the brokenness. We are invited both when we are in a good groove and when we cannot hold it together for even one more moment. We gather when the despair and loss are overwhelming and we simply need to be reminded that we are loved. When we can no longer hold everything ourselves, the gathered people of God remind us that we do not have to.

What does the church do when we gather?

Woven together in moments momentary and lingering
    to worship God,
    to know what it is to belong,
    to celebrate the jubilance of life,
    to grieve when life is loss,
    to lament and to confess,
    to forgive and to be forgiven,
    to worship, to pray, to march, to nap,
    to argue, to ponder, to weep, to laugh,
    to discern the mind of Christ and the will of God,

*to love the other as the world would not want us to love
ourselves,
    to affirm and proclaim that we belong to one another,
and in turn we belong to God.*

Opinions about what we're supposed to do when we gather as the church run the gamut. Some churches focus on political and social activism, working toward social liberation and institutional change. Other churches aim to be a place where you can sit and open yourself up to the Spirit, build an awareness of God, and develop a relationship with the one called Jesus, both individually and communally. Sometimes these two kinds of churches turn on each other.

This battle—you could call it the Justice or Jesus battle—has raged for generations, with each side criticizing the faith of the other. I've always felt like these two approaches are intrinsically connected. If we don't hold together these ideas—the church as a place of justice and service and activism, and the church as a place of spiritual growth and connection to Jesus—then we miss out on the gifts of both.

So the list in the faith montage section above summarizes the things that we are called to be and do in the church. The church can be so spiritually powerful because we do not have to do all those things alone. At any one time, somebody may be praying when somebody else cannot pray at all; some may feel excluded while other folks feel like they belong; some may be weeping while others are laughing. The church can be active in many ways, but ultimately it's not the activities or the programs or even the community that makes the church worthy of our time and energy. We gather together to discern the mind of Christ and the will of God and to commit ourselves to living these values in the world.

God calls us into a relationship filled with love, trust, and justice. A discerning community finds ways that the world needs us. Churches offer people the chance to lament and rejoice, to forgive and be forgiven, and to go through the rhythms of life in a way that brings freedom and liberation.

If the same God, why so many churches?

We gather in forms and functions as expansive as creation is itself,
*   by affiliation, association, denomination, and affinity*
*   in living rooms, kitchens, coffee shops, corners,*
*   country churches, town-square sanctuaries, grand cathedrals,*
*   amid blaring speakers, bright lights, sacred windows, shiny*
*   screens,*
*   pipes floor to ceiling, folding chairs, dripping candles,*
*   well-worn pews, and worn-out carpet,*
*   with cymbals, bells, lyres, guitars, organs, drums, soundtracks,*
*   and turntables.*

One of the first questions that new-to-the-church folks often ask is, "What's up with all of the different churches?" At first glance, the fact that so many churches and denominations exist does seem slightly off. What about this "unity in Christ" that Christians hold so dear?

This is an understandable place of confusion. But it makes sense that there are as many manifestations of the church as there are ways of being human. Some churches gather around a shared cultural experience, some gather because of geographic proximity, and still others because a conflict forced a larger network to split into multiple communities. Not all denominations and networks are for everyone, and some differences create deep division.

Yet the fact that different denominations exist allows people to find the right place at the right time in order to grow in faith. I do not see the existence of denominations as a sign of division or human failure. I choose to see the breadth of Christian expression as one way that the Spirit expresses God's love of diversity, even if we do not always understand or agree with it.

I write out of a deep commitment to denominational church life. At times in my career you could have called me a church bureaucrat and not been wrong. My home denomination, the Presbyterian Church (USA), depending on your context, has been at times conservative, at other times liberal, and always everything in between. My denomination, while one that is generally recognizable (but often misspelled), is just one of many.

Some believe that the era of denominations and associations is over—that monolithic entities no longer fit a culture of transience that has folks of all ages moving more than ever. Can one-size-fits-all entities like the Methodists and the Presbyterians and the Baptists meet the needs of contemporary people with a craft-beer sensibility? Maybe not. Yet I do not believe that denominations have outlived their effectiveness. Like many other things in the world—technology, money, food, sports—the church itself can be good or bad depending on what function it plays in our lives.

God gives us agency, and we get to seek out particular communities that feed us and bring us joy. Ultimately, to be part of a church, denomination, association, or network is to acknowledge that one particular community cannot be all things to all people. This is not a negative or divisive reality; rather, it is an opportunity to work together. The burdens of the world are great, so the more we can embrace the benefits of our denominational or churchly life, the more we can rejoice in the work that we do together.

What does it mean to be church?

Basking in the sounds of invitation.
Held in welcomed silence.
God gathers us still.

Whether you are exploring church for the first time or have seen the behind-the-scenes reality of how the church operates, choosing to be part of a community is just that: a choice. If a church doesn't provide us with a sense of belonging, if it doesn't feed our soul, if it doesn't help us to be good participants in society, and, ultimately, if it doesn't help us become more like Christ, then why bother gathering? If you are exploring becoming part of a worshipping community, I encourage you to ask these questions.

A healthy community acknowledges that each person has a finite amount of energy, resources, and skills, and it embraces the reality that we carry one another through life. I do not have to do things all on my own. I do not have to carry the weight and the energy all on my own. To be fully church together means trusting that God has somehow cobbled together this misfit community so that, through us, God can do amazing things.

Possibly the most important reason that I am part of a church is that it challenges me to grow in my relationship with God. Being part of a community of faith prompts me to look inward: to reflect on my areas of brokenness, sorrow, or despair, and to find ways to know healing and hope. The church also challenges me to look outward: to understand my place in the world, my privilege, and how the resources I have can do good in the world. The systems of the world would rather that we hoard all that we have and be driven by a mindset of scarcity and self-preservation. The church, at its best, rejects destructive individualism and reminds us of God's great abundance, not only in our material resources but also in our capacity to care for one another.

For all these reasons, and because I have seen the church at its best, I commit to this thing called church, over and over again.

REFLECT

Individual: When was the last time you gathered with people across seemingly differing contexts? What was the common draw?

Communal: How do you embody and express invitation, welcome, and belonging?

Practical: What denominations or associations of churches have you connected with, and what makes them unique?

Montage: What are three beliefs that you have about who and how God gathers?

BREATHE

Inhale: "Gathered by love,"
Exhale: "We gather to love."

Four

Hurting

Deep in the first year of the COVID-19 pandemic, suffering, death, and loss were taking over. With thousands of deaths every day, thousands of families and communities had to ride wave upon wave of grief. The politics of the time were enraging and violent. Across the globe and across political parties, we were battling over vaccine mandates, mask-wearing, and whether Covid was even a real thing. The politicization of the pandemic led to far more death and suffering than would have occurred had we come together to pursue the common good and global health.

A racial reckoning also came to a head after the murder of George Floyd by the Minnesota police. The Black Lives Matter movement gained momentum, defunding the police became a priority for many, and antiracism work finally entered into mainstream culture and politics. Still, many folks continue to reject any attention to systemic racism, police brutality, and white supremacy.

On December 11, 2020, my grandmother, May Chow, died from complications of COVID-19. Because the pandemic was ravaging the world, we could not be with her. This meant that, with a stranger holding a tablet in front of her, three generations from across the country gathered to say our goodbyes to her through our screens.

This is not the way it should have been. I wrote her a letter the day after she died, and I have read that letter many times since she left this earth. Each time I weep. Each time I am transported back to that time, and I feel once again all the grief and anger over how she had to die.

I weep frequently, and not just when a loved one dies. I angry-cry all the time. This trait was passed down from my grandfather to my mother to me, and I have passed it along to my children. We wear our emotions right out there, and when we see injustice in the world, our righteous indignation often manifests in tears of rage. We do not apologize for these tears even when they get the best of us, for these tears water the soil from which our commitment to healing and wholeness grows.

I can only imagine the depth of weeping that God does when they see how humanity wreaks havoc upon creation and one another. We have given God more than enough reasons to weep. Which brings us to our next topic: sin.

Now before you throw this book across the room with an exasperated, "I knew it! This is just another 'you're a sinner' book! I thought I could trust you, Bruce!" hear me out. In order for Christians to participate in the healing of the world, we must acknowledge the ways in which we have instigated, participated in, and reinforced pain, violence, and trauma. By doing this, we give ourselves a shot at drawing nearer to God. Ignoring our complicity in the pain of the world means furthering our separation from God.

That is what sin is: a separation from God. It's a separation instigated not by God but by us, as humans—a separation we create through our intent or apathy. Yes, the word *sin* has been weaponized by many. Sin drags a huge set of social and theological baggage behind it—baggage that needs to be unpacked. Maybe some of us will never fully redeem or reclaim sin as a word in our vocabulary of faith. But we still have a responsibility to pursue a relationship with God and to seek God's hopes and intentions. And that means holding ourselves accountable when we move further away from fulfilling those hopes and intentions rather than nearer.

Call it what you want—sin, brokenness, depravity, whatever—most of us can agree: humans can be terrible. We need only look at how we inflict pain upon one another and the earth. And while we may be tempted to gloss over sin because we want to get to the forgiveness part of the Christian story, we must reckon with sin if we want to be part of any healing—our own or the world's.

What is sin?

But these called, sacred, gathered bodies are HURTING.

*From ancestors and saints past to misfits and strangers of today,
we live in a world that feeds on destruction, rewards hatred,
reinforces oppression, dismisses grief, denies accountability, and
manipulates vulnerability—
and often in the name of God.*

We have lost our way.

Christians often get stuck on the concept of sin. Some Christians focus so much on it that they can't see outside of how conservative Christianity has cataloged sin, and they end up weaponizing it against vulnerable people. Other Christians ignore how often we and others turn away from God—so much so that we lose sight of our own shortcomings, the fact that we are constantly reinforcing systems that bring pain to the world.

Sin is, put simply, any act or thought that turns us away from God's intentions. Sin encompasses all the ways we intentionally turn away from God's purposes for humanity.

The problem is that Christians often try to define exactly what acts and thoughts constitute sin. That's where you get into the litmus testing, with people trying to determine whether you are sinful or not. Again, that's not what I'm talking about when I talk about sin. I'm talking about any act or thought that leads to, contributes to, or reinforces situations of oppression, violence, pain, suffering, and separation from God.

Again, you don't even have to use the word *sin* if it's a block for you. But even if we avoid the word, we can't avoid the fact: we all do things that separate us from God's intentions for humanity and for the planet.

How does sin manifest itself today?

We have turned and been turned away from God's intentions and hopes for humanity.
We have brought pain upon my body, your body, our bodies.
Born from anger, disappointment, and mourning,
God weeps with and for me, with and for you, with and for us.
    As we desecrate the earth, God weeps.
    As we equate light as good and dark as bad, God weeps.
    As we pursue profit and perpetuate poverty, God weeps.

*As we criminalize suffering and incarcerate siblings to
invisibility, God weeps.*

As we fortify empire and exploit humanity, God weeps.

As we legislate bodies and deny human agency, God weeps.

As we mock emotions and renounce empathy, God weeps.

*As we choose individualism and abandon the common good,
God weeps.*

As we worship "normal" and demonize difference, God weeps.

*As we benefit from unjust systems and justify their existence,
God weeps.*

As we deny privilege and default to indifference, God weeps.

As we choose apathy and forsake the body politic, God weeps.

*As we profit from disparity and blame others for their
desperation, God weeps.*

*As we deny the sins of our past and reinforce institutions of
oppression, God weeps.*

Our sin manifests itself in small and large ways, and always with community and global impact. As I wrote this section of my faith montage, I wanted to name *all* the things we do that turn us away from God's intentions without diluting the power and the impact of naming particular places of struggle. Essentially, when there's brokenness in the world—when violence is inflicted upon bodies, when institutions reinforce oppression, and when sin is lived—God weeps.

God takes the side of the suffering—those who are suffering in body, mind, heart, spirit, or soul. God not only takes the side of the suffering; God weeps when we bear the brunt of violence, oppression, and poverty brought about by condition, circumstance, or even choice. This includes everything from very personal issues around racism, misogyny, ableism, queerphobia, and xenophobia to how we address large issues like climate justice, border militarization, global security, and distribution of wealth.

There's enough blame to go around. Not only must we take responsibility for the ways in which we individually sin against one another; we must also take seriously the fact that systems and institutions of which we are all a part create suffering. In taking responsibility, we turn toward God's hopes rather than further away from them.

Sin exists. We can call it what we want, but pretending that we do not play a part in it only reinforces that which we may claim to stand against. By refusing to name sin as a force in the world, we refuse to see reality as it is. So we need to name the sin, name the brokenness, name the ways we inflict pain upon ourselves and others, so that we can seek and experience healing.

A quick word here about evil and hell: If you search my faith montage, you will see that it does not touch on evil or hell. That is intentional. It's not that I do not believe in either; I do. Rather, it's that neither are formative aspects of my faith. Yes, I believe evil exists and manifests itself through individuals and institutions, and I believe we must fight evil with love and cultivate spaces less hospitable to evil's growth. As far as hell is concerned: Conceptually, I believe in a state of being in which one is cut off from God's presence. I believe that it is a state of being more than a place of existence. And I have little interest in trying to figure out what or where hell is, whether people end up there, and if they do, how or why it happens. My energy is better spent on embodying and expressing hope, rather than debating the reality or roster of hell.

How does our sin impact others?

And as we embolden violence upon bodies
  who bear darker skin,
  who go unheard,
  who believe differently,
  who love who they love,
  who are deemed weak,
  who are silenced,
  who are unarmed,
  who are not in control,
  who broaden gender,
  who are gifted to our care,
  who are the "enemy,"
  who are different,
God weeps.

Every single one of us—at different levels and with different motivations—inflicts violence on other human beings. We all enact emotional, physical, and spiritual violence upon one another. None of us are immune to the human instinct to survive, which means we don't always think about the impact an action will have on another person.

We have to name the ways we individually inflict violence upon other human beings and how we do so over and over again. That's called confession. Because we are not perfect, we will return to the well of destruction time and time again, even after having visited places of healing and restoration. No matter how small the infraction, how contrite we may be, or the relative impact upon others, when pain and suffering are experienced, God weeps.

The church must respond to acts and words that strip humanity from others, and we must stand with those who are targets of suffering and oppression. We must name the pains of the world—some of which the church itself has caused—and we must fight for the dignity of all creation. God has told us that all human beings have been created and are beautifully and wonderfully made. We must reject the impulse to debate anyone else's humanity.

God weeps when people inflict violence upon one another. God weeps when people question the equality of others because of their skin color or their gender or who they love. We have taken those prejudices and institutionalized them, not only in government or the corporate world but also in the church. We as individuals must acknowledge any part we play in reinforcing oppression and suffering and then change our ways.

Why are lament and confession essential?

We resist and refuse to lament and confess
to that which holds us back from fully knowing God.
Born again and again from anger, disappointment, and mourning,
God weeps.
And yet.

To lament means letting ourselves feel, to the depths of our souls, the pain and suffering in the world. Lament tells us that, before we jump to confession, we must examine how we have perpetuated pain and suffering. Lament also forces us to build up our capacity for empathy so we develop a greater appreciation for the humanity of those who surround us. Only by sitting in lament are we able to move into confession: to let go of those thoughts, actions, and intentions that hold us back from God and to take hold of a new life filled with healing and hope.

Some churches include a time of confession in every worship service, and many people wonder why. Doesn't confession just make us feel bad about ourselves? Doesn't it leverage guilt and shame in an unhealthy way? Others wonder about the value of confession done by a group of people. When confession is done corporately, it can't reflect all the individual sins that exist in a space, can it?

These are good questions. But I believe that confession, when done well, does not simply produce shame or guilt; it releases us to the possibilities of reconciliation and healing that can only come *after* we understand that we need to heal and be reconciled. Too often we want to move past confession and rush to absolution. We want to rush to being forgiven for what we have done so we can feel okay about ourselves again. No one wants to admit to wrongdoings in their lives, no matter how insignificant, but it paves the way for healing.

When we hold up a mirror to our own sinfulness—which is essentially what we do when we confess our sins—we sometimes do end up falling into guilt and shame. But if shame and guilt are our only motivations, any change in behavior lasts only as long as the shame and guilt are present. To be clear, I do not argue for a confession that does not motivate us to change; rather, our motivation should be a deep yearning to own our sins enough to change our behavior in the future.

So instead of beating ourselves up about our sin, we can ask: What effect has my sin had on another? How might my yearning to have other human beings feel dignity and humanity connect to my need for confession? And then, in response to those questions, we begin to live differently in the world. We begin to find the grace of God, which helps us avoid repeating our sins and find a new way.

REFLECT

Individual: How do your individual actions reinforce hurt in the world?

Communal: In what ways are you part of corporately reinforcing hurt in the world?

Practical: What are a few ways you may change to a posture of healing?

Montage: What three beliefs do you have about how God's gathered are hurting?

BREATHE

Inhale: "When we hurt,"
Exhale: "God, you weep."

Five

Healed

My spouse and I met when I was eighteen. We were engaged a year later and married by the time I was twenty-one. On the surface, this may not seem problematic. But back in those days, your boy Bruce here did not inspire confidence in the maturity and commitment departments. I had never dated anyone longer than six months, I had just escaped a felony charge for reckless driving, and I had only recently decided that binge-drinking was not the best way to ensure a long life. Now I can see why many of my family and friends were a wee bit concerned. A few years into our marriage—which has now lasted thirty-plus years—they were almost proven right.

I was in North Carolina at a youth conference and had time on my hands. I had always wanted to get a tattoo, so a friend and I found this great tattoo parlor/gas station. Let that sink in: a combo gas station and tattoo parlor. We met with the tattoo artist the day before so he could show us his ballpoint-pen-and-model-plane-engine combo tattoo needle and we could show him the designs that we wanted to permanently place on our bodies. At twenty-three, I was still not particularly mature, but I did know enough to run this idea past my spouse. So I called Robin and let her know that my friend and I were planning on getting tattoos. I don't remember her words exactly, but the sentiment was clear: she would prefer that I didn't. Not hearing a literal no, however, I went off to that tattoo parlor/gas station with an illustration of a Celtic cross that I'd ripped out of a church catalog, and I got that tattoo on my ankle.

When I returned home, you could say that I was not warmly received. Hence we entered one of the most trying times in our marriage. No degree of mental gymnastics on my part could counteract the reality that the majority of the blame for my poor decisions belonged squarely on my shoulders. I hadn't listened to my partner and had proceeded to act solely out of my own needs and wants. I see now that I was hurting not only my relationship with my wife; I was hurting my relationship with God. More than thirty years later, I'm grateful that we sought reconciliation and that I never messed up again. Okay, that second part is a lie. We have both messed up plenty, although less frequently as we have matured. But when we do, we return to the discipline of discerning God's intentions together. Today, as then, we share in healing when we are hurt, and in doing so we both grow closer to one another and closer to God.

Sin—the human proclivity to forget and turn away from God—is deeply personal and massively global. It is as intimate as the selfish actions of a young spouse and as public as the systems of oppression in which we all participate. And as much as I would love to believe that humans fundamentally want to help others find healing and wholeness, sadly, I believe that our commitment to the healing of individuals and society extends only as far as our own comfort, security, power, and financial well-being allows. Sometimes the world seems unable to move, blanketed by a low-grade fever, weighed down by depression, or in too much pain. Sometimes this pain exists because of the sinful nature of productivity culture, the drive to accumulate wealth, or the fact that we don't love our bodies. And at other times, sin shatters the very landscape of our world, as cities are devastated by war, creation is ravaged by pollution, and children die in a hail of gunfire.

I know that this sounds pessimistic, but just think about it. If those of us who possess and pillage the majority of the earth's resources stopped, and if we could find a way to redistribute wealth, food, education, and healthcare, we could alleviate global poverty and the suffering that is widespread throughout the globe. We could make the same case about personal protection and comfort, about guns, body image, worth, and other personal issues. We often lack the imagination or the will to see a reality beyond our own comfort. But imagine if we chose to step into generosity, abundance, and care of one another and the earth. I have no doubt that we would all know healing beyond our imagination and grow closer to God. Believing in a future of healing defiantly proclaims to the hurt, hate, and despair of the world, "You shall not have the last word!" Choosing faith means believing that the healing, love, and hope of God will.

What do healing and wholeness mean?

And yet we know what it is to be HEALED.

To be healed is to be whole.
To move toward healing is to move toward holiness.
In mind. In body. In gut.
In heart. In spirit. In soul.

ealing is difficult to describe, but we know when we feel it. It's like a weight has been lifted off your chest, or like you have finally exhaled a breath that you've been holding. That moment of unspoken love between two partners, after a festering disagreement is past and trust is reclaimed: this is healing. That moment of reconciliation within a family, after unhealthy patterns of behavior are acknowledged: this is healing. That moment of understanding within a community, after patterns of division and conflict are addressed in ways that allow for growth and acceptance: this is healing.

In these moments, your body, mind, and spirit often feel something holy. That, for me, is what it feels like to be healed and whole. Healing is often difficult to define, but we know it when it happens.

Can we experience healing on our own?

You cannot be healed if I am still hurting.
I cannot know wholeness if you are still in agony.
We cannot experience either while neighbors and strangers suffer still.

My wholeness is intricately and intrinsically woven together with yours and yours with mine.
Healing is mine is yours is ours.
Wholeness is ours, is yours, is mine.

---

ealing is tricky because it is so often tied to our relationships with others. It is difficult to achieve healing in isolation. The pursuit of healing and wholeness is not a mandate to stay in relationships that cause the hurt in the first place. But when possible, addressing hurt collectively is a powerful path toward healing. When we know healing, we no longer find ourselves or our relationships driven by pain and conflict. When we know healing and wholeness, we no longer approach our relationships with timidity, hoping simply to avoid conflict; rather, we embody confidence and trust, and we support those around us in their pursuit to grow into who God hopes them to become and to grow as close to God as possible.

It is in these moments of reciprocal support when I feel most healed and whole and when I know that God is with me and God is with us.

How do we experience God's healing?

Yet we cannot know healing and wholeness without the One who loves us into being.
  God loves healing into the world.
  In whispers. In whimsy. In wonder.
  In exhale. In excitement. In euphoria.
  In solitude. In silence. In subtlety.

Our bodies, minds, and souls are healed by God.
  Healed in ways creative, soothing, beautiful, and bold.
  Healed in ways surprising, subtle, unruly, and old.
  Through boisterous laughter uncontained,
    and anger righteously expressed,
  through sounds that soothe
    and silence that settles,
  though communities organized
    and justice realized,

through intimacy, generosity, understanding, and rest,
through equity, jubilance, remembrance, and risk,
through lament and confession,
through forgiving and being forgiven,
through grace offered and grace accepted,
through being seen, being heard, being known.

I wish there were a "Top 10 Ways to Be Healed by God" list out there somewhere. Personally, I'm sure it would include "eat bougie avocado toast," "buy more hats," and "cuddle all day on the couch with your dog." And while those may indeed bring me healing, there simply is no officially God-reviewed and -approved list. Each of us, depending on the situation and our context, will experience healing in different ways. Healing may change from time to time and from situation to situation. In the specifics of our heartache and in our healing, we must discern God's hopes and intentions for us.

The important thing is to be open to how God may be reaching out to heal us. Sometimes, in our pursuit of healing, we inadvertently create more hurt. When we tend to our own healing, we must not allow our self-care to turn into an abdication of responsibility to participate in the healing of others. Experiencing God's healing means embracing how each of us best experiences healing. For some, healing is about changing patterns of unhealthy behavior, such as our relationship with food or online engagement. For others, it may mean reengaging past practices like meditation or prayer. For some, it may mean stepping away from a particular person or situation; for others, it may mean recommitting to a person or place. And yes, it may even mean eating bougie avocado toast, buying more hats, and cuddling on the couch with your dog. In the end, healing happens best when we are attuned to God and the unique ways in which God heals each of our souls.

Why do we need God's healing?

In all of these things,
in God's good time,
in unexpected ways,
God's healing and wholeness is a mighty balm
    for our bone-tired bodies,
    for our compassion-fatigued hearts,
    and for our weary, weary souls.

Again, I can't prove to you the reasons God should be at the center of your healing. But I do know that immense depths of pain and despair require immense depths of healing and hope. I believe that the healing we need comes from God.

Yes, I value all the ways that humanity has learned to heal the body and mind through science, medicine, psychology, therapy, and the like. But healing is not an either/or endeavor: that is, either we are healed by God, or else we are healed by modern medicine. One cannot be fully known without the other. Without modern approaches, we may miss out on treatments that would do us great good. But without understanding the deeper spiritual elements at play, interventions run the risk of becoming temporal and fleeting rather than transformational and sustained. Knowing that the healing of our souls works in concert with modern-day science gives us access to a healing and wholeness that goes beyond our greatest hopes.

REFLECT

Individual: Where in your life do you most need to know healing
and how might you get there?

Communal: Where in your communities is healing most needed?

Practical: How might you extend an act of healing to someone
who might not expect you to care about their hurt?

Montage: What are three of your beliefs about God's healing?

BREATHE

Inhale: "Our hurt is deep."

Exhale: "God, your healing is deeper."

Six

A Few Words about the Spirit and Us

As a young pastor in my first church assignment, I quickly became frustrated with the system, I felt sabotaged by some folks in the church, and I felt underappreciated for the growth that I had helped to lead. I was so stressed, and my body was so exhausted, that I developed a heart murmur. After just four years in that first pastoral job, I resigned, thinking that I had, for all intents and purposes, left professional ministry. I threw a massive pity party for one, and no one else was invited but me, myself, and I.

So as an almost-thirty-year-old, I began working in retail, at an upscale hippie health and wellness store in San Francisco that sold candles, essential oils, and homeopathic medicines. I enjoyed doing customer service, but I was always thinking about my calling to ministry. The church that I had pastored had grown pretty quickly, and I missed preaching and leading worship. I especially missed walking alongside folks during their journey of life and faith. I did not, however, miss the immovability of organizational structures, the arguments over music styles or flower placement, and the way a new idea could turn rapidly into a battle of wills. I needed a break, as I had grown more than a little bitter and resentful. Not ideal traits for a pastor.

After about a year of talking about my bad experience of pastoring with anyone who would listen, a mentor of mine, Bert Tom, sat me down. When I first met Bert, he seemed kind of crusty and prickly, but as I got to know him, I saw that he was a pastor at heart, caring, compassionate, and warm. I count myself fortunate that Bert cared for me enough to push me.

Burt was very clear about what he thought God has in store for people. One day, when he had invited me out to lunch, he skipped all the pleasantries and, with language more colorful than I can write here, said, "Okay, Bruce. Are you done whining about the church yet? And are you ready to get back to work?"

In that moment, it was clear that the Spirit was speaking. (Also clear: having a mentor can be a real pain when you just want to wallow in self-pity.) It wasn't the spirit of gentle winds and cool breezes. This was a Spirit who poked and prodded relentlessly, and in the places that I least wanted to be poked and prodded. Sometimes the Spirit makes us uncomfortable and pushes us to ask ourselves questions that we would not otherwise choose to ask, let alone answer.

In the next set of chapters, we'll look at the nature of the Spirit, as well as at the multitude of ways that the Spirit guides, informs, compels, and draws us into textured and living faith.

How does the Spirit move?

I choose to believe in the activity of the Spirit, moved and moving.

The Spirit, sometimes known as the Holy Spirit or Holy Ghost, is the main catalyst for God's movement and growth in our faith, in our lives, and in the world. Language about God can be confusing, but know that there is no ranking or hierarchy to God. God the Creator is fully God, Jesus is fully God and fully human, and God, the Spirit, is fully God, manifested in living movement in, with, and among humanity. It can be confusing, for sure. But ultimately, the power of God is in God's ability to be all of these things all at once.

The Spirit can be sweeping and audacious, like fire, breath, and wind. The Spirit can also be subtle and nuanced, acting as wisdom, counsel, and awe. Throughout the Bible we see various ways that the Holy Spirit moves, especially in the life of Jesus. The Spirit impacts the life of Jesus: "The Spirit of the Lord is upon me, because the Lord has anointed me. He has sent me to preach good news to the poor, to proclaim release to the prisoners and recovery of sight to the blind, to liberate the oppressed, and to proclaim the year of the Lord's favor" (Luke 14:18–19). The Spirit also speaks to those who follow Jesus: "I have spoken these things to you while I am with you. The Companion, the Holy Spirit, whom God will send in my name, will teach you everything and will remind you of everything I told you" (John 14:25–26).

The Spirit does a multitude of things: compels us into action when we need prodding, reminds us of the presence of God when we forget, and invites us into places we might not go on our own but where we meet God more fully. The Spirit is the inspiration and sustenance that fills our hearts, our bodies, and our souls with energy. The Spirit is God's persistent prompting and prodding for us to grow into who God wants us to be.

At times the Spirit is compelling, speaking to us beyond our rational ways of thinking, beyond the voice in our head that says we can't, or we shouldn't, or we daren't. The Spirit's messages to our souls are often beyond explanation and sometimes beyond rationality. The Spirit manifests itself by unapologetically moving our minds, hearts, and souls to do something new. In these moments, the prompt is not simply "Would you like to do this?" or "Have you considered that?" It's much more urgent than that. The Spirit inspires us to work not off our timeline but God's. When the Spirit moves, we move.

At other times the Spirit is a gentle nudge to go forth—a longing for the beautiful and the true, an urge toward the good. The Spirit shows up when we need encouragement, or a loving nudge to get us over that hump of resistance, apathy, worry, and anxiety. The Spirit often offers that last little bit of encouragement when we are hesitant about going into a new space or getting to know new people or starting to serve the world in a new way. The Spirit gives us the gentle push we need to enter into the possibilities that God is revealing.

If it sounds like the Spirit demands too much, never fear: the Spirit also sustains us. We can only survive on inspiration for so long, and an invitation only lasts until we accept it. In a culture that always demands more, more, more, the Spirit offers us sustenance for the journey. Sometimes the Spirit reminds us that it's okay to step away from spaces that demand too much of our energy; sometimes the Spirit whispers in our ear that it's okay to rely on the assistance of others; at other times the Spirit screams at us to slow down, rest, and take a long afternoon nap covered in a blanket of puppies.

The Spirit doesn't just call us into new spaces and then leave us to fend for ourselves; the Spirit reminds us that we are not doing this on our own.

REFLECT

Individual: What have you been taught about the Spirit?
Communal: How is the Spirit most known in your communities?

Practical: Can you recall an instance when the Spirit was clearly active in your life or someone else's?

Montage: What are a few beliefs that you have about the Spirit?

BREATHE

Inhale: "Spirit, sustain me."

Exhale: "Spirit, send me."

Seven

Inspired

Rev. Dr. J. Alfred Smith, senior pastor of Allen Temple Baptist Church in Oakland, California, was one of the most powerful preachers in the country. When I was in seminary in the 1990s, he taught preaching. During the first class, he asked us, "How many of you want to preach like me?" Of course we all raised our hands. Why else would we be there if not to learn how to preach like Rev. Dr. J. Alfred Smith? We already know how to preach like *ourselves*. Silly Rev. Dr. J. Alfred Smith!

Apparently he had different plans. In one of our early classes, he explained that we were going to try a preaching exercise. He would read a random Scripture passage and then ask one of us to stand up and preach on that passage. I looked around, trying to detect if anyone else was as horrified as I was. This was not what we Presbyterians did! In my tradition we prepare. We exegete. We most certainly do not just get up and preach off the cuff.

So when he asked if there were any volunteers, all of us brave seminarians looked down at our desks. Rumor had it that Rev. Dr. J. Alfred Smith could smell fear. When one classmate made the deadly mistake of looking up, it was all over for them. Dr. Smith called the person up, read a passage from the Bible, and said, "Preach!"

It was extremely awkward at first. Our classmate stammered and stuttered and generally looked as terrified as we would have felt. But as Dr. Smith coaxed and coached the student through the process, our classmate became more animated and confident, finding insights in the Scripture passage and rendering them in plain language, clearly and concisely. It became clear to all of us that the Spirit was moving. By the end of the class, it was evident to all of us that we had to learn to trust the Spirit. The Spirit will move alongside and despite us; we just have to believe this to be true.

This is true not just in preaching but in life. Trusting in the Spirit allows us to approach even the most daunting of tasks with a posture of inquiry and possibility. While we may not always be sure about our capacity to try new things, we do not have to sell ourselves short. Of course, no one person can do everything or be an expert on all things, and we do not want to overestimate our abilities to the detriment of others. But we can begin any new endeavor by trusting that the Spirit will draw out the gifts that we ourselves may have yet to discover.

How does the Spirit inspire, move, and accompany us?

The Spirit of God repeatedly sweeps over humanity, leaving us INSPIRED:
> *to seek God's hopes for each of us,*
> *to live into God's intentions for the entire body,*
> *and to answer the call to participate in the fulfillment of God's ever-revealing hopes for the world.*

The Spirit invites us into relationship and conversations with God. The Spirit encourages the quest and reveals God in the act of questioning.
The Spirit pokes and prods us to be open and aware that God is with us.

The Spirit revives, refreshes, and reminds us that God will help bear the weight of our weariness.

L et's get more specific about how we may notice the Spirit's activity. It can move when you are still and listening for God; you could be outside, listening to the ocean waves, listening to the breeze through the forest, or simply sitting on your front stoop, listening to the sounds of your neighborhood. The Spirit can speak, even loudly, as you're walking down a city street or stuck in traffic on the way to work or to pick up the kids from school. There is no one way that the Spirit moves.

In fact, the Spirit often moves on the least expected individuals and communities. Essential to the work of the Spirit is the element of surprise. Sure, the Spirit may move when we want it to and when we plan: when we gather for worship or do churchy things like make decisions about budgets and buildings. But often the Spirit moves simply when we gather over a meal or a service project, or when we hang out in the parking lot, or when we bump into one another at a soccer game or a café. While there is no one way that the Spirit moves, we do know that the Spirit moves.

Why is the Spirit important?

The Spirit is unwavering in the belief that we have the capacity to know God more.
The Spirit moves around us.
The Spirit moves through us.
The Spirit moves in spite of us.
And when we are open, the Spirit moves us.

The Spirit is a reminder of our capacity to know God more tomorrow than we did today or yesterday. The Spirit relays God's message to us: that God trusts and believes in us, and that we can live into God's greatest hopes for us.

So even when we get in our own way, and even when we try to dodge the call or block the Spirit, God says, "I still trust that you will listen and that you will respond." The Spirit is at work not because of our unwavering belief in God; the Spirit is at work because of God's unwavering belief in us.

REFLECT

Individual: When has the Spirit inspired you by surprise?

Communal: How does your community leave room for the Spirit to show up?

Practical: Read a random Bible text, a poem, or another spiritual reading, and then share with someone what it means to you.

Montage: What are a few beliefs that you have about the timing of the Spirit?

BREATHE

Inhale: "I trust in the Spirit of God."

Exhale: "The Spirit of God trusts in me."

Eight

Storied

In times of great tragedy, even preachers don't know what to say. Sometimes we get caught up in trite sayings or theological platitudes and end up doing damage to grieving people. While the intention may be honorable, telling someone that the death must be "all part of God's plan," or that their loved one is now "in a better place," results in trauma for many. Such attempts at explanation tell a story that God has inflicted pain upon someone. This is not the version of God that I believe to be good. This is a masochistic God: a divinity who deserves to have people turn and run the other way.

In 2009 I had to preach the most difficult sermon of my life. A few weeks earlier my brother-in-law, Brian Pugh, had been shot and killed at a workplace shooting in Santa Clara, California. I was tasked with organizing, planning, and leading his memorial service, which was both an immense honor and a heart-wrenching burden. When I got up in front of family and friends after my brother-in-law's horrific death, I wanted to be clear that I didn't believe his death was part of some divine plan. "None of us should be here," I said as I began my sermon. "*God* does not want us to be here."

As we explore how God's story is revealed, I hope that we can move beyond the simplistic narrative that everything happens according to God's plan and that there is always a Bible passage to irrefutably answer every question. I hope we can move beyond seeing God as a manipulating puppeteer. What if God actually trusts humans' capacity to navigate the complexities of the world? What if God's story unfolds through us?

What does it mean for God's story to be revealed?

The STORIED revealing of God's hopes and intentions is intricately woven
in and through our interactions with God—
a delicate conversation between Creator and created.

When I talk about God's story in these chapters, I am referring to something different from what most people mean when they talk about "God's plan." I reject the notion that everything happens for a reason as just plain false. I do believe in the beauty and power and perfection and truth of God's story, in its unfolding and revealing nature. And I believe that God's story will someday be fulfilled. Make no mistake: God is the driving force of history, the present, and the future.

But God's story is not done or finalized. It's also not the only story being acted out in the universe. The unfolding of events in our lives represents an ongoing conversation between the Creator and the created. It's a conversation—a call and response, a give and take—that allows for both God's movement and human agency. The fullness of God's story for us all is being made known, but it is always partial, and it is always in conversation with us.

We will not always recognize God's story as it is being revealed. But, thankfully, God has left some tools to help us discern God's ever-revealing story for the world. Thankfully God does not simply plop us down on this earth, hand us a bagged lunch, and wish us good luck in figuring it all out. God still speaks to us; always has, always will. Today God speaks through Scripture, through prayer, and through the lives of ancestors and saints, past, present, and future. God speaks to us through friends, family, colleagues, and strangers, and always through the ongoing movement of the Spirit.

The goodness of God tells us that there *is* a story that will be revealed. But that is different from a belief that "God's plan" means something predetermined, divinely directed, specific, and even coercive. I believe, instead, that God invites humanity to play a part in God's story.

We get to listen for the many ways God speaks to the world, to question that which needs to be challenged, to shift when the Spirit beckons us in a new direction, and to embrace our roles as co-conspirators with beauty and truth and justice and goodness. God's story unfolds in the revealing and realizing of God's plans for the world.

How does the Spirit move through prayer?

The Spirit moves through prayer:
Not a checklist but a conversation.
Not performance but release.
Not to control but to relinquish.
Not to manipulate but to listen.
Not with words but also with words.

Simply put, prayer is a conversation with God. Whenever I'm in conversations with people, I ask myself: What is my role? Is it to simply listen, or is it to respond? Is the person asking for counsel and advice, or do they simply need a sympathetic ear?

When it comes to prayer, which is our conversation with God, we can ask the same questions. We lift every prayer to God for a different reason and with a different mindset, and God responds in different ways. Sometimes prayer is one way: we talk and God listens. Other times we are the listener, silencing ourselves long enough to hear from God and detect the movement of the Spirit.

Exactly how you pray is up to you. Some folks engage in a regular discipline of prayer at a particular time each day, while others see prayer as more spontaneous and interwoven with our activities during the day. I think a healthy prayer life includes a bit of both. We should all set aside some time to focus our body, heart, and mind on listening for God; we also need to be open to the moments when we simply need to talk to God or God needs to talk with us. No matter how or how much we pray, we can rest in the knowledge that God is paying attention. God's capacity to hold and respond to all things is far greater than ours. God responds to us in surprising and mysterious ways. The Spirit is at work as you and I converse with God.

How does the Spirit move through community?

The Spirit moves through community:
   Not to demand but to discern.
   Not to fix but to encourage.
   Not to confine but to compel.
   Not to detach but to engage.
   Not to seek perfection but to love perfectly.

No one likes to be told what to do. One of the most difficult aspects of being part of a church is discerning God's will for one another. None of us wants a group of people to be all up in our business. But a community of faith can be a discerning, thoughtful presence that helps us truly determine God's intentions. Too often our American culture of individualism means we are not bound by any communal understanding but driven by the desire for personal power and wealth. God often speaks most clearly when a group of people gather: to struggle through conflict, to acknowledge multiple gifts, and to come out on the other side. Together, in community, we can grasp a deeper understanding of God's intentions than we can on our own.

When we are part of a community, we learn when and how to make our voices known. Are we that voice tenderly whispering in the background or the one boisterously cheering others on? Are we the voice that constantly speaks in solidarity with those who are silenced? Are we part of a chorus of voices shouting and chanting because the concerns of the oppressed are not being taken seriously? Or are we the ones who focus our efforts on listening deeply to others? The Spirit will speak through us in different ways at different times, and the Spirit is made known to us through the voices of others.

How does the Spirit move through the Bible?

The Spirit moves through the Bible:
    Not an indifferent collection but an anthology of human
    experience.
    Not a contract to be enforced but a covenant to be honored.
    Not a map to be followed but an adventure to be embraced.
    Not a literal set of rules but evolving truths to be revealed.
    Not a weapon of faith but a wellspring of liberation.

The Bible tells the breadth and depth of the human experience with God. The Bible both liberates and binds; it is a living conversation and delicate dance between humanity and the Spirit. It's a record of God's story as told by authors who sought to discern God's movement in the story of their people. Yes, it contains beautiful passages that evoke love, hope, joy, and peace. But the Bible also contains the rawness and reality of a world filled with ugliness, despair, sorrow, and destruction. While some prefer a faith devoid of difficulty, strife, and conflict, I find deep comfort in the fact that, in the midst of the good and the bad, God still speaks.

I do not deny that the Bible has been weaponized to oppress communities, justify systems of violence, and otherwise serve as a handbook for human havoc-raising. But I am not going to start there. I want to start with why I believe the Bible is important. Put simply, the Bible operates as a living guidebook for our lives. The Bible guides us into understanding God's faithfulness to us. While some see Scripture as clear and concise rules for life, I don't. In fact, the Bible is anything but clear or concise. But I do believe that reading Scripture challenges us to dive into discerning God's longings for us, in any particular time and circumstance.

Most importantly, the Bible communicates God's greatest hopes and intentions for humanity. The Bible is long and complicated enough to embody a multitude of God's hopes for us. When we read the story of Jeremiah, in which God calls a child to speak truth to the world, we might find God calling us, too, to be prophetic in the face of injustice. As we read about Jesus's constant prayer and study (which often left the disciples confused), we might commit ourselves to practices of self-reflection and discipleship, which means following Jesus. In Mark 2, when we read of people going to great lengths to carry their friend to Jesus for healing, we learn what it means to experience belonging. Through the wisdom literature—Job, Psalms, Proverbs, Ecclesiastes, and Song of Songs—we are given language for God's beauty, creativity, and expansiveness. Through the Bible, God tell us through human authors, "Here is what I hope you to be and become, and I am with you always."

As much as the Bible brings clarity, it is also filled with contradictions. Using a lens of biblical literalism—the belief that the Bible is the exact word of God—to understand a document written by humans is fundamentally flawed and leads to proof-texting and dangerous misapplication.

If you are willing to take the text out of context, you can probably support almost any position, about anything, by using the Bible. The weaponizing of the Bible is one of the most destructive and dangerous parts of Christianity, past and present. For instance, when people claim "biblical marriage" as the standard in the debates about same-gender marriage, they do so as if there is a singular standard of marriage endorsed by the Bible, and thus by God. News flash: if we listed the ways in which people engaged in marriage in the Bible (polygamy, incest, sexual violence, and an absence of state-sanctioned marriage at all), most people would not choose to have a "biblical marriage." This is where the Spirit comes in, challenging us to interpret Scripture in community and to hold onto nuance. The Spirit reminds us that, even though this text was written by human hands, over generations, and through countless cultures and contexts, the words are as alive today as they were when chisel, quill, or pen was first put to stone, parchment, or paper.

Seeing the Bible as a living, breathing container of God's voice to us is not a sign of weakness or an old-fashioned, out-of-date faith. Rather, it is a sign of depth and confidence of faith in God's meaningful presence yesterday, today, and always.

How does the Spirit inspire, surprise, and strengthen?

The Spirit moves in the in-between:
Not always knowing where but trusting God is present.
Not always knowing how but trusting God is active.
Not always knowing when but trusting God is near.
Not always knowing why but trusting God is faithful.
Not always knowing but trusting that God is.

Through these windows
we meet ourselves,
we meet others,
our understanding of God is expanded,
the movements of God are made real,
and the revealed and revealing story of God is made known.

The Spirit is wily and surprising, popping up in unexpected and surprising ways. We do not want to live like we're in some horror movie, waiting anxiously for the Spirit to jump out from around the corner with a shriek and a boo. Rather, the surprise that the Spirit brings is often well beyond our imagination. Tenderly, we remain open to these surprises: from the most intimate of our relationships ("What will our life together look like in the future?"), to communal discernment ("How will we participate in the ongoing movements for justice in the world?"), to everything in between.

The Spirit invites us to be stretched and shaped so that we may have a deeper, broader understanding of who God is. Reading God's story, and becoming part of it, means opening up our hearts, our minds, and our spirits to see God in new and powerful ways. When we can be open and receptive, we grow closer to God and more fully live into God's hopes and intentions for us all.

REFLECT

Individual: What are some of your biggest questions about the Bible?

Communal: How have you experienced communal prayer?

Practical: When have you seen the Spirit move you or a community to action?

Montage: What are a few things that you can say you believe about the Spirit?

BREATHE

Inhale: "Spirit, you are speaking."
Exhale: "I am listening."

Nine

Compelled

My maternal grandmother, Marie Averas, was what you might call a firecracker. She was determined, opinionated, and honest, loyal to her family and friends and adventurous of spirit. My mother was just like her, so it is no surprise that she and my mother had a tumultuous relationship. There are so many stories to choose from, but the most startling one involves my mother, at sixteen, slapping my grandmother during a fight. At the time, my grandmother walked away—but she did not forget. You see, our family has Olympic-level grudge-holding skills. Two years later, when my mother turned eighteen, my grandmother's birthday gift to her was moving boxes.

Soon after that, my mother gave birth to her first child (Hello me!). She contemplated giving up custody of me. When my grandmother got wind of this, she wrote my mother a letter designed to convince my mother to keep me—and it worked. I still have the letter. I know that, for some people, being placed for adoption is the right thing for parent and child, but my grandmother felt otherwise.

My grandmother likely didn't want to write that letter, but I think she felt compelled to do so. She overcame whatever barriers would have stopped her from putting pen to paper—pride, frustration, busyness, worry about her daughter's future as a single mother—and she wrote those words of persuasion. And I'm so glad she did. My grandmother helped to reveal a pathway before my mother—the possibility of keeping me—that she may not have otherwise seen. By writing that letter, my grandmother became a collaborator with God, an accomplice with the Spirit.

The compelling Spirit moves us into places where we have the opportunity to grow closer to God. The Spirit cannot physically force us to enter a given situation; to be *compelled* means that we sense an internal beckoning that will not let us *not* move. There is no rhyme or reason about where we may be compelled to move. Sometimes we may be compelled to reengage a situation with which we have deep history; other times we will be compelled to step away from relationships that are no longer good for us; still other times we may be compelled to enter entirely new spaces. Yet no matter where we go, the Spirit will be with us.

Why does the Spirit compel us to go into the world?

It is into the revealing story of God that we are COMPELLED to go.

> *Where we are called to serve God and others.*
> *Where we are drawn into a deeper relationship with God.*
> *Where we are thrust into the struggles of the world.*

It is in God's revealing story where we grow into who God intends us to become.

Not if we go, but as we go.
As we go, we seek:
    Wisdom. Healing. Growth. Love.
As we go, we are healed:
    By others. By ourselves. By surprise. By love.
As we go, we offer back to God:
    Our talents. Our resources. Our humanity. Our love.
As we go, we share what and who we know God to be.
    Hope. Joy. Peace. Love.

We have to be connected to others if we are to experience the fullness of the Christian faith. We can grow spiritually as individuals, yes, but only to a certain extent. While private spirituality may provide temporary satisfaction, we must also make ourselves aware of the realities of the world, which often happens in community. Often, when church people talk about "mission," we mean going out into the world to share what we know of God, frequently in service of others. We take part in the journey toward healing by offering what we know of God's healing. That said, when we engage with any community—church, neighborhood, movement, place of service—we must be careful not to enter with a savior complex or the belief that we have all the answers. Rather, we must open ourselves up to the possibility that God may be calling us to be vulnerable, and to be teachable, and to choose faith by learning from the faith of others.

Even talking about "mission" and "sharing the gospel" and "going into the world" is fraught. I get it: many of us are afraid of becoming *that* kind of Christian, the one who assumes that other cultures, people, and traditions are in need of "saving"—by us. So we hold back, fearful of being perceived as—or actually *being*—patronizing or condescending. (More on this later.)

Humility and restraint are great instincts. But I also think that *not* sharing such an important part of our lives—our faith—deprives others of the beautiful version of faith that they may have never heard of. Think of groups of people who gather around a common hobby or a concern for a cause or a shared love of a place: How do these groups share their mission and vision and eagerness that others will join them? Can we learn from their enthusiasm and their method, which is often rooted in a hope that others will find meaning and purpose as they have? In fact, when so many know Christianity only as hateful and divisive, what a relief it will be for others to know that, in your experience of God, there is love and hope! In our attempts to avoid reinforcing colonial, oppressive forms of Christianity, we end up burying a better version of the gospel under a bushel. What if everything good about God is true? This better version of faith might be just what others need in order to experience healing.

Of course, we all make mistakes. We all stumble and make conversations about God more awkward than they need to be. That said, I hope that, with the confidence of our loving God, we will trust that we will lead not with misguided arrogance but with a faithful confidence. We can trust the Spirit who calls us to step into the world in the first place. We can trust the Spirit that I believe compelled my grandmother to write that letter to her daughter—a letter that literally changed my life.

As we open ourselves to the Spirit, we may feel compelled to share this version of a relationship with God with those who are desperately seeking it.

REFLECT

Individual: How comfortable are you in sharing your faith with others? Explain.

Communal: How do communities around you, faith-based or secular, share their mission and vision?

Practical: What interest, passion, or belief have you shared with someone else?

Montage: What are a few things that you believe about sharing faith in the world?

BREATHE

Inhale: "Spirit, if you send me,"
Exhale: "I will go."

Ten

Revealed

We always want to know why bad things happen. It's like we think that if we know why a tragedy happened, we will know who to blame—or even better, how to avoid it the next time. Many Christians engage in excruciating theological gymnastics to justify or explain why good things happen: that God has rewarded us for our faithfulness, or that everything that happens is somehow all part of God's plan.

While I understand the motivation to explain away pain with tidy theology, I think we are better off walking a humbler path, one that acknowledges that sometimes beautiful things just happen and sometimes traumatic and terrible things do. The more important question, for me, than *whether* bad things are part of God's plan is *how* we understand God's intentions for good in the world. Sometimes choosing faith means discerning God's presence in the midst of things we do not understand.

In the summer of 1987, I was getting ready to leave home and head to college. I had been accepted to the University of California at Irvine, about a seven-hour drive away. Preparations were in full gear: my roommate had been assigned, I had begun selecting classes, and I had just broken up with my girlfriend because I was "not ready for a long-distance relationship." Good lord, I was melodramatic.

So many changes and transitions were ahead of me. I was excited for college and ready to begin the next stage of life.

And then I got a call from my dad.

For years, the understanding was that he was going to pay most of my college expenses. My mom had raised me on child support of fifty dollars a month (welcome to 1970s single motherhood), so it always seemed fair that college would be his turn to really step up. One day he called me and cut right to the chase: he didn't have the money to pay for college. I could not believe it. Looking back now, as a parent, I cannot imagine how difficult it must have been for him to make that call. That day, however, I was devastated, and I could not see beyond my own anger and disappointment. I had already begun saying my goodbyes to friends (imagine my ex's shock when she found out I *didn't actually leave*). My plan—from high school to university to law school to a career in politics—was derailed.

Fast forward thirty-five years, and here I am, with college and graduate education behind me. I'm doing just fine professionally, emotionally, and personally. Am I still holding some hurt from that experience? Yes. But my professional and personal trajectory, birthed directly from that disappointment, has led me to this point in my life, for which I am deeply grateful. And with all my heart, mind, and soul, I believe that God's Spirit has been present around, throughout, and amid it all.

I share this story *not* to reinforce the idea that one has to suffer hurt or trauma just so that God's path may be revealed. I do not believe that there is one singular path for any of us. But I do believe that God moves *with* us no matter where we go. I do not believe God thinks so little of us as humans that God moves us around like chess pieces in some grand, universal game. Humans have more agency and creativity and smarts than chess pieces, and I choose to believe that God does too.

I do believe that God has a plan that is being revealed and that this plan is made up of God's deepest intentions and fondest hopes for the world. But God's intentions and hopes are not the same as direct maneuvers. They are simply that: intentions and hopes. We as humans can align ourselves with those intentions, or we can run from them. We can try to discern God's invitation and accept it, or we can give ourselves over to distractions.

Our role is to discern how we are to respond to the invitations that stand before us. It's not some existential guessing game, in which we must unlock the answer to one singular unknown-to-us-but-predetermined-by-God destination. Rather, following the Spirit throughout our lives is a journey of discernment: one that allows us to grow as humans, as siblings to others, and in our relationship with God. *That* is ultimately God's plan.

How do we look back on God's presence in the past?

As it has been with generations before and will be for generations to come,
God's story has and will be REVEALED to God's gathered people.

I try not to judge how other pastors do their work, but my super-judgey gene gets activated when I hear or see pastors doing things that I think are dangerous and hurtful for those they are called to serve. One of my pet peeves around pastoral care is the phrase "everything happens for a reason." As I've mentioned, I believe that it is a dangerous theological concept. Believing that God had a "plan" that generations would have to suffer argues against the God of love and hospitality in whom I choose to believe.

I think about my own grandparents and their immigration story: my paternal side from China in the 1940s and my maternal side from the Philippines in the 1930s. While it is tempting to define their lives solely based on the sacrifices and suffering they endured in order to make a path for generations to come, I do not believe that struggle was part of any plan by God. Yes, they survived those years. But the racism and exclusion that they encountered should not be construed as some kind of gift from God. We can lift up their experience in order to make sure no one else has to go through that experience, but we should avoid romanticizing their oppression.

I believe struggle and despair can be transformed into liberation and hope. Our ancestors often listened for God through the struggles playing out all around them, and that faith defined them. The gift of the past is not that people learned to suffer through some plan orchestrated by God. Rather, seeing how our forebears lived out God's story in the midst of their suffering helps us to seek God in the midst of ours.

How will the story be revealed?

The story will meander,
but God's time is God's time.
The story will confuse,
but God will guide us if we choose to follow.
The story will contradict,
but God's perfection lies in a willingness to change.
The story will be deemed weak,
but God reimagines what is powerful.
The story will seem like a distant figure emerging from the mist-worn fog,
but when we see God, we really see God.
And we will know.
The story will be revealed.

B ut how, Bruce? you ask. How do I know what God's story looks like for me, for us, for my community, or for the world? Sadly, I don't know. I wish I could tell you that the story will be revealed in a text message, delivered by certified mail, or dispatched via skywriting. But that is simply not how it happens.

I am generally not patient enough to wait to move forward until I receive clarity and confirmation of a direction, so I often storm right ahead, hoping that I am following God's story. Sometimes this works out just fine; other times I end up making poor choices. Yet in both "good" or "bad" choices, the grace of God is present. There is always space to discern which path is of God and which is not. Sometimes diving in, without knowing all the details of what God hopes, is how we participate in the unfolding story of God.

I believe that we discern God's intentions best with a community. With others, we are able to reflect on happenings, ask clarifying questions, and discern the mind of Christ and the will of God. We get teased a lot in my tradition, the Presbyterian Church (USA), for our committees. And it's true: group work like committees and commissions and study groups can be time-consuming and frustrating to no end. But I remain Presbyterian because those processes challenge me, encourage me, and hold me accountable to the discernment of other Christians. The discipline of discerning God's story in a group of people forces me to acknowledge that I do not have all the answers, that others can expand my worldview, and that ministry is more meaningful when undertaken with others.

God's story is revealed to us as we listen deeply. We listen for God's voice in both subtle and surprising ways, for God's guidance when shifts in perspectives are calling our names, and for God's encouragement when the path meanders. All of this will test our patience and trust. But when we undertake the discipline of seeking God in all that we do, we can find a spirit of calm in a world of chaos, a posture of deliberation in a time of constant change, and the strength of community in a time of rabid individuality.

The revealing of the story of God takes many forms. And while that answer may disappoint those who want one exact reason why good or bad things happen, I take heart from this truth: that God trusts us. God trusts us to find our place in the multitude of stories being revealed all the time.

Yes, we can learn to trust God more and more over a lifetime. But if God trusts *us*? Well, that might just change everything.

REFLECT

Individual: What have you been taught about "God's plan"?

Communal: How have you seen God's story being revealed in communities of which you are a part?

Practical: Name a situation or experience that you now believe was part of God's revealed story.

Montage: What are a few things that you believe about God's revealing story?

BREATHE

Inhale: "Sometimes I am lost."

Exhale: "Spirit, guide me home."

Eleven

A Few Words about Jesus and Us

Finally we get to Jesus: the center of this thing called Christianity. Other religious traditions may respect and acknowledge Jesus as a good person or a prophet. But the Jesus that Christianity centers is Jesus as fully human, fully divine, worker of miracles, raised from the dead, and now sitting at the right hand of God (Matthew 16:19). For most Christians, it is Jesus the Christ who is our central and unique connection to the divine. It is around and through Jesus that the rest of our faith grows.

The Christian communities that formed me focused on Jesus as a historical character, a wise teacher, and an example of how we should live in the world and treat people. I grew up in a tradition that was mostly about a communal relationship with Jesus. This stands in contrast to some traditions, evangelicals foremost among them, that focus mostly on a "personal relationship with Jesus Christ as Lord and Savior." They emphasize what Jesus did for us on the cross and encourage us to see Jesus as our friend.

I was raised in northern California, and to our progressive liberalism that phrase (a "personal relationship with Jesus") set off alarm bells. Saying anything close to that probably meant that you were one of those right-wing, conservative, fundamentalist Christians. In my church we steered clear of that language, and I sure did not want to be known as one of those "Jesus people" or as a "Jesus freak."

Those alarm bells are not without merit. The idea of "a personal relationship with Jesus" has been used as a litmus test for faith, and it has manipulated, harmed, and frightened people into a faith built on shame, guilt, and fear. Yet I'm sure that many Christians would say our understanding of Jesus, inside the progressive church circles that raised me, was so communally oriented that it lost all salience for our individual lives and choices. They might point to the way that many progressive churches are hemorrhaging youth to suggest that we didn't emphasize the importance of a personal choice to follow Jesus.

For far too long and in too many places, these two perspectives have been seen as mutually exclusive. We have set up a binary: "communal relationship with Jesus = liberal" and "personal relationship with Jesus = conservative." All this goes to show that one of the least helpful things the church can do is to advocate for *one* ideal type of relationship with Christ. We must not act as if there is only *one* way to be in relationship with Jesus—as if our personal relationship with Jesus and our communal relationship with Jesus can somehow be separated. Our communal and individual relationships with Jesus are connected, and each loses out when they are not known by the other.

In the next few chapters, Jesus takes center stage. I hope you will trust me to take you through a more complex, beautiful, and liberating introduction to this person Christians understand to be fully human and fully divine. This person of Jesus—who lived, died, and was resurrected in ways that connect us to God for eternity—offers us multiple ways to move through the world with courage, empathy, discipline, and creativity.

One of the best ways to learn about Jesus is to read Matthew, Mark, Luke, and John, the books of the Bible called the Gospels.

Taken together, these four books illuminate so much about Jesus's life and teachings, as well as how powerless people were drawn to him and powerful people often felt threatened by him. Reading or rereading these books is a good place to start as you think about Jesus.

Who is Jesus Christ?

I choose to believe in grace made real through Jesus Christ.

For the complete and complex humanity of Jesus,
and the mysterious and boundless divinity of the Christ

Oh, we have so many questions when it comes to Jesus! What did he actually look like—and does it matter? Can't we just follow his teachings and not worry about the "fully human, fully God" stuff? What about all this salvation talk, with a parent sacrificing their only child (what the actual eff)? And resurrection: Are we talking about actual bodily rising from the dead? Oh, and communion, with the eating and drinking the body and blood of Christ: seriously?

We will get to salvation, resurrection, and other concepts related to Jesus soon. But let's begin with talking about who Jesus is. First, it is important to acknowledge that when we try to define who Jesus is, he often ends up looking and believing and acting a lot like us. I hope to offer a framework for understanding who Jesus is and also examining the understandings we bring. Naming who we *think* Jesus is can help us both clear away some of our own preconceptions and also notice the various ways that Jesus meets us.

Let's begin with some questions that help us figure out what we think of Jesus. Consider which of these statements seems right to you.

A. Is Jesus a Prophet, a table-turning activist and political troublemaker who challenges us to express our righteous indignation with passion and courage?

B. Is Jesus a Priest, a going-off-to-pray miracle worker and spiritual teacher who offers us a way to connect with God?

C. Is Jesus a Pastor, a giving-the-benefit-of-the-doubt curator of relationships and bridge builder who yearns for us to cross cultural, economic, and theological divides?

D. Is Jesus a Poet, a more-questions-than-answers sculptor of words and actions, one who opens the human imagination to see possibilities for the world?

Like so many multiple-choice tests you took in high school, I believe the right answer is actually E: All of the Above.

Naturally we tend to focus on the aspects of Jesus that we like and shy away from or reject those parts that challenge us. If we are activists, we likely focus on the prophetic nature of Jesus. If spiritual disciplines are our jam, we focus on the priestly aspects of Jesus. If relationships are the most important part of our faith life, then the pastoral Jesus is where we find connection. If we like using our imagination about what life could be, bring on Jesus the Poet! Expanding our understanding of Jesus might challenge us to consider who Jesus is calling us to be—and then we might have to adapt, change, and respond!

This idea of the fourfold nature of Jesus—Prophet, Priest, Pastor, and Poet—is not new. It has roots in the writing of John Calvin, a French theologian who lived during the Protestant Reformation of the sixteenth century. Even though I disagree with Calvinists about a lot, these frames help me embrace the breadth of who Jesus is rather than focus on the parts I like. Sure, we will all gravitate toward one or two aspects of Jesus's life and teachings—a part of him with which we feel a special bond. But we must not do so to the extent of ignoring the other aspects of Jesus, who models for us the importance of holding in harmony the ways we move through the world.

Let's look at each aspect more closely.

How is Jesus Prophet, Priest, Pastor, and Poet?

The prophetic Jesus is the activist, the one who wears passion and anger out in the open. The Prophet Jesus is filled with righteous indignation because humanity has lost sight of who God is calling us to become. Prophets do not predict the future of the world; they express to the world God's intentions for its future.

The priestly Jesus tends to our connections to the Holy One, to God. He calls us to a life of prayer, reflection, worship, and spiritual discipleship. The priestly Jesus reminds us to stay rooted in our divine connection and calling and to continue to follow the one who has called us. Jesus does this not out of a need for control but a yearning for us to also have integrity in what we do. This priestly Jesus acknowledges the need to keep growing, learning, and inquiring, because we are never done becoming what God intends. In many ways the perfection of Jesus shows up in his willingness to admit imperfection and continue to learn, grow, and better follow the calling of the Spirit. Jesus the Priest helps us see and connect to God's guidance and growth, not our own.

The pastoral Jesus challenges us to be in community, even and especially with those who are excluded, hated, or plain impossible to love. Jesus pushes us to reimagine what it means to offer a place of belonging. Relationships are not just about being nice, avoiding conflict, or sacrificing convictions to find commonality; rather, they mean seeing the other as divinely created, beautifully complex, and always in process. By following the pastoral Jesus, we remember that other people are created by and also belong to God. The Pastor Jesus does not demand conformity and uniformity from those who claim to follow him, but rather empathy, compassion, and understanding.

And finally, the poetic Jesus. Rather than pushing us toward a faith that is stifled, calcified, and boxed in, the Poet Jesus offers us a revelatory and expansive faith, fueled and fed by divine imagination. Jesus the Poet is not a beret-wearing hipster reciting spoken word in a darkened café. Then again, he could be. The Poet Jesus could also be the trans soloist in a church, offering operatic beauty to the world. The Poet Jesus could be a bisexual Latinx living off the grid in a tiny home, challenging the world to rethink our relationship with the land, its people, and ourselves. The Poet Jesus could be the teenager hiking three miles into the desert to drop water, food, clothing, and medical supplies to help save the lives of migrants who are making the dangerous trek across the borderlands. The Poet Jesus could *be* the migrant making the dangerous trek across the borderlands. The Poet Jesus shows up at the church potluck, at the musical concert, through the latest smartphone app, in our alone time, and places too numerous to count.

Are these the only images for Jesus? Surely not. But they are a place to start. Noticing these dimensions of Christ pushes us toward a nuanced and whole version of Jesus that provides a footing for future exploration of faith. These images free us to think about who Jesus may be for each of us, rather than providing a confining narrative for who Jesus must be for everyone.

Putting Jesus into a theological, social, cultural, or behavioral box is exactly what fundamentalist, conservative Christian traditions do. So let's not do that. Rather than using Jesus as a rigid litmus test for proofing and proving beliefs and behaviors, we must allow Jesus to guide us. Jesus, in all the beautiful breadth that is possible, leads us as we move together toward a more just, wise, and loving world.

REFLECT

Individual: What are some of more recent things you've learned or heard about Jesus?

Communal: How does your community understand or talk about Jesus?

Practical: Of the four natures of Jesus, toward which one do you most gravitate?

Montage: What are a few things you believe about Jesus?

BREATHE

Inhale: "Christ, the one called Jesus,"
Exhale: "Good to meet you."

Twelve

Grateful

My wife and I have been married since 1990. If you remember my story about the tattoo, you may be surprised that we have made it this long. Lots of people are. The full story of our marriage is a story for another day, but the primary emotion I feel when I look back on more than thirty years is gratitude. Gratitude motivates me to choose every day to be committed to this person.

Our children tease me that I'm soft and emotional and kind of a hopeless romantic; when pressed, I might even confess to believing in that outdated notion of "soulmates." I do not want to risk ridicule from my kids, so I'll just say that I am exceedingly grateful that somehow, so many years ago, Robin made room for me. I'm grateful that she supports me in growing into the person God hopes that I become. That gratitude compels me to try to be a supportive spouse, an attentive partner, a nurturing parent, and a humble, just, and kind human. Each day, when I choose to try to be more present and loving today than I was yesterday, and when I choose to honor the commitment that I have made to Robin, I am doing so out of a deep and deepening sense of gratitude.

Similarly, as we learn to discern God's hopes and intentions, we can reject doing so with a transactional spirit and can do so from a place of gratitude. Shame, guilt, and obligation are not sustainable motivations; they are short-term tactics driven by proximity to fear.

So as we explore who Jesus is, we begin with gratitude. Gratitude is crucial, for we live out our faith in response to what Jesus has *already* done, not for what we expect Jesus to do for us.

Who was Jesus—and who are we?

I am GRATEFUL.
Grateful for the prophet, activist, and agitator,
    who speaks God's hopes, intentions, and truth into the world.
Grateful for the pastor, protector, and gatherer,
    who curates space for curiosity, compassion, and kinship.
Grateful for the priest, steward, and guide,
    who tends, grounds, and guides the spirits of those on the
    journey.
Grateful for the poet, artist, and creative,
    who instigates, inspires, and invites exploration of divine
    possibility.

This lens of Prophet, Pastor, Priest, and Poet invites us to think more broadly about the nature of Christ and to be changed and transformed by each. As I mentioned, we are naturally drawn to the aspect of Jesus that most mirrors our own personality or preferences. I know that I lean toward Jesus the Prophet: the activist and the rabble-rouser, because I believe that protest is an essential aspect of most movements for change. It's taken me a while to appreciate how different people follow Jesus. But being open to the fullness of the ways Christ calls us expands my understanding of the nature of both Jesus and myself.

Here are a few examples of how Jesus manifests these four ways of being.

Jesus the Prophet: In John 4, Jesus talks to a Samaritan woman at a well. At first glance, this seems to be a simple act of kindness. But given the systems that marginalized her because of her gender and social standing, this was an act of protest.

Jesus the Priest: In Matthew, just after he and the disciples somehow fed five thousand people, Jesus goes away to pray and sends the disciples out on a boat. This is not just about Jesus needing to take time for himself to rest; it is about challenging the disciples not to revel in their own abilities to make miracles happen but to remain centered on the power of God.

Jesus the Pastor: Jesus is constantly inviting people into spaces of belonging and community. In Matthew 11, Jesus calls those who are weary and reminds them that in following him, and in belonging to this movement, they will find rest.

Jesus the Poet: Throughout Scripture, Jesus answers accusations and questions with stories and more questions. This approach is not about abdicating responsibility or trying to shame somebody. He tells parables and poses questions to challenge us to think more expansively and creatively about our faith.

I am not always receptive to the challenge of embodying the multidimensional expressions of Jesus. Sometimes I want to be prophetic when I really need to be pastoral, and sometimes a priestly posture is not as helpful as a poetic one. But at the end of the day, I am always grateful for the many ways that Jesus challenges me to see the importance and interdependence of each.

Why is the humanity of Jesus so important?

*Grateful for the unpretentious life of Christ,
    the teacher and friend.*

M any people like to see Jesus as a friend: somebody who plops down beside us, puts their arm over our shoulder and just gets us. There is great comfort in the human Jesus . . . *and* there is so much more to who Jesus is.

While we do not know much about his early years, we know that Jesus felt sad when friends betrayed him. He got angry at injustice and oppression and expressed empathy in the face of accusation. He knew joy at the growth of others and lost hope when he felt abandoned by God. All the things that make us the complex, beautiful creations that we are—Jesus experienced them as well. Knowing that Jesus felt the heights and depths of human emotion means we can find with him a friendship, a kinship, a siblinghood, and a shared reality.

Why are the life, death, and resurrection of Jesus so important?

*Grateful for the revelatory death of Christ,
    the offender and threat.
And grateful for the promised resurrection of Christ,
    the seeker and solace.*

*For in the life, death, and resurrection of the one called Christ,
    we are reconnected to God,*

reunited with the saints,
loved for eternity,
and promised that one day there will be a new heaven and new
earth.

Some traditions skip over the death and crucifixion of Jesus and head right to Easter and the empty tomb. In a world filled with so much pain and struggle and strife, I understand the urge to skip over sorrow and get to the good part. But the death of Jesus is the culmination of a life that challenged institutions of power, questioned authority, and rejected exclusionary norms—to the point where he was killed by those whose power he challenged. If we take the death of Jesus seriously, we must examine our own institutions, power, and norms and see if they too must be challenged. The death of Jesus shows us that anyone who brings attention to institutional sins or challenges the authority of the powerful risks suffering and death. The death is a mirror of what can happen when power is threatened, so we must not skip over it too quickly. If we do, we risk siding with the powers that Jesus stood against in the first place.

The death of Christ also offers us a connection to God. While the death of Jesus was not a requirement for God's love, it provides a moment when God, through Christ, experiences the depth of human suffering. This moment joins us to God in a way that goes beyond any act or teaching of the living Christ. Jesus's death inextricably and eternally bonds humanity and God in a way that only shared death and suffering can do. Ultimately, the death of Christ, and the despair that those who believed in him felt, provided God with an opportunity to exhibit hope and new life.

You have probably heard the words *atonement* and *salvation*. There is no one right understanding of the atonement (how the sins of humanity are absolved) or salvation (how humanity is eternally connected and saved as God's own). Penal substitutionary atonement theory says Jesus was offered up by God in place of humanity to pay for our sins. Christus Victor theory says that Jesus's crucifixion was an act of victory over sin, evil, and death. The moral example theory says that the death of Jesus offers humanity an example of what it means to follow God, even to one's death.

There are far too many theories of atonement and salvation for me to tackle here. Instead of focusing on atonement theories, I want to suggest to you that the *life* of Christ has just as much to say as his death and resurrection do. The healing that Jesus offers to so many—the grace and forgiveness that he extends, the hope that he offers his followers—is too powerful for me to ignore. These were not acts of a mere mortal but divine revelations of new life, abundant hope, and eternal connection to the divine. Do not let anybody tell you that there is one *right* way to believe about the atonement or salvation. Rather, rest in the belief that even when we do not know the hows or whys, God has promised that death and despair will not have the last word.

So what about the resurrection of Jesus? (A theology of the resurrection in a few hundred words? Sure, no problem.) Let me start by saying that I believe in the bodily resurrection of Christ. Betcha didn't see that coming! I mean, I've been sounding like a thoughtful person, and now I'm admitting that I believe that a dead body can come back to life? Exactly.

It is important for you to understand this: I believe in the bodily resurrection not because of science or empirical evidence but *because* it is an outrageous and disruptive claim. It is an event beyond my imagination and beyond my human comprehension, and, if true, it turns upside-down my assumptions about the future of the world. But it's that very fact—that it transcends everything I assume to be true or possible about how the world works—that gives me hope.

Working in concert, the life, death, and resurrection of Jesus talk back to so many indicators that suggest that death and destruction will have the last word, that the world is destined to crumble. The bodily resurrection of Christ gives me hope that, through the power of God, the world can become better. I choose to believe that the world will know healing beyond what I as a mere human can comprehend.

Salvation is about an eternity of connection to God. It is not about saving anyone from a lifetime of damnation. You do not need to believe that salvation is experienced solely and only through death on the cross; you need not see Jesus connecting us to God for eternity as some militaristic or conquering victory; and you certainly do not need to believe that salvation is the result of some divine parent sacrificing their child. What I offer to you is the possibility that salvation is an expression of love, an act of hope, and an unearned promise. Jesus didn't die just as a sacrifice for your sins; Jesus lived and was resurrected for the hope of your future. No matter how despairing and broken the world is, the life, death, and resurrection of Jesus promises that we are connected to God for eternity and that hope, joy, love, and peace will have the final word. In gratitude for this promise, we worship and serve God in our lives and the world.

Why does a belief in Jesus matter?

For this I am grateful.
For this we are grateful.
In all of this, we find mystery, meaning, and motivation.

So when it comes to an answer to the question "Why Jesus?" don't give up on the question simply because the answers you may have heard so far aren't satisfactory. Don't assume that someone else's answer to that question has to be the same as yours. Personally, I do not believe Jesus is the only way to meet God or the only way to salvation. While I don't believe that Jesus is the only way for everyone, he is a life-giving, beautiful, and worthwhile way for me and many others. In Jesus, I find a pure and powerful calling to be a human worthy of the love God has promised me. Through Jesus's life, death, and resurrection, I am connected to God now and forever.

Choosing faith each day, for me, means claiming Jesus as my ultimate guide, teacher, sojourner, comrade, collaborator, and accomplice. Jesus provides a complex and complete example of how I strive to live in the world. Some traditions motivate with obligation, shame, and guilt; following Jesus in those ways seems exhausting, miserable, and demotivating. Rather, because of the depth of humanity that Jesus experienced, the divinity in which he lived, and the unimaginable act of coming back to life, in gratitude and joy I choose Jesus as the one to trust, follow, and lean on throughout all my days.

REFLECT

Individual: What troubles you most about the way that you have heard others describe or define Jesus?

Communal: How does your community best express its understanding of Jesus?

Practical: When was the last time you heard someone explain the crucifixion as something *other* than Jesus dying for your sins?

Montage: What are a few beliefs you have about the nature of salvation and resurrection?

BREATHE

Inhale: "Jesus, for your life, death, and resurrection,"
Exhale: "I am grateful."

Thirteen

Generous

When our kids were young, one of our favorite family activities was going to the animal shelter. We'd walk through the rows of puppies, kittens, dogs, cats, and other creatures for an hour or two, talking with the animals and petting them and playing with them when staff allowed it. Our children, now young adults, have fond memories of those visits.

Want to know the real reason we took our kids to the animal shelter? We could not afford to take them to the zoo. For a long time when our children were young, we could barely pay for groceries, special lunch items, or field trip money. We lived near plenty of family, so we were never in danger of being unhoused or going hungry. But when we lost our home and moved our family of five into a two-bedroom, one-bathroom apartment, we did it out of necessity, not because we wanted to downsize. We were in poverty.

We are in a much better financial situation now. Robin and I have always tried to be appropriately transparent about our financial situation with our kids, so as they moved toward adulthood, we let them in on the fact that, for much of their childhood, we lived under the poverty line even though we were both working. Only then did they realize that some of the things that we did when they were young were not because we were cool or creative but simply because we were poor.

I would never say being poor is good for people, or that struggle is the only way one gains perspective. These are both problematic postures toward those who have no choice in the matter. But our kids see the world through a different lens than many of their peers do. I think growing up with very few extras has made them more compassionate and empathic. For example, we don't joke about any restaurants being "low class," because we remember the days when going out to eat—even for fast food—was a special occasion. We don't shame people for making bad food choices, because we know what it is like to eat bean soup five days in a row because that's all you can afford. And we certainly do not judge people by the cars they drive, because we know what it's like to have a car break down and have no idea how you will drop your kids off at school next week.

Again, we had supportive family around us, so we had the privilege of knowing that we could borrow money, move in with someone, or otherwise avoid having to make life-endangering choices. At the end of the day, we always had enough. Even when we were struggling, we tried to model being generous with what you have. We taught our kids that the point of life is not to accumulate or hoard but to steward wisely what you do have. We tried to follow God's call, trusting ourselves to make good decisions and believing that, in doing so, all would be okay and that we would have enough.

Simply put, we can be generous because God has been generous to us.

We don't give our time, our energy, and our talents so that God will love us more. We are not generous because we are trying to earn something or because our generosity will somehow make God treat us better than that schmuck on the corner. We are generous because of the generosity of the resurrection. We respond to the needs around us because God has promised to love us not only now but throughout eternity. We respond in the world as if that gift matters. The resurrection compels us to be generous.

Each day, as we tune ourselves toward God's hope for the world, the Spirit reminds us to be generous because God has been generous to us.

Why should we be generous—and why is it so difficult?

I believe in the GENEROUS spirit of God.

God has been generous to me, so I give back to God
*   all that I have the courage and faith to offer.*
When the fear of scarcity causes me to forsake abundance,
*   I choose generosity.*
When the insidiousness of convenience causes me to avoid discomfort,
*   I choose generosity.*
When capitalism makes me want to commodify what I offer,
*   I choose generosity.*
When arrogance causes me to tie strings to my gifts,
*   I choose generosity.*
When despair causes me to ask, "Why bother?"
*   I choose generosity.*
When I forget that I have chosen to believe that, in life and in death, I belong to God,
*   I choose generosity.*
I choose generosity because God has been generous to me.

Placing this chapter on generosity in the Jesus section may seem odd. Yet I want to argue that the abundance of life that we are given by Jesus's life, death, and resurrection can change how we live. Out of the gift of new life, humanity is compelled, commanded, and convicted to be generous: generous beyond our imagination and beyond the expectations of the world. Radical generosity flows out of the idea that there are enough resources for all of us to thrive.

Being generous with our time, talents, and treasures is not easy, because the idea that we would ever have "enough" is a foreign concept in a culture driven by reckless capitalism and the myth of meritocracy. The world tells us there's never enough, especially when it comes to money, wealth, prestige, and power, and that we should always seek more. I reject this. We should only use what we need—nothing less, nothing more. The life, death, resurrection, and salvation of Christ means that whenever we have more than enough, we can be generous.

A note about the idea of "enough": it is relative and contextual. When our family talks about "enough," it is very different from conversations among those who are on the verge of losing housing, facing food insecurity, or facing bankruptcy because of medical bills. I do not take those situations lightly. Some of the most generous people I know have been living on the edge more than most middle-class folks can imagine.

Scarcity and abundance conversations are complicated because the economic chasms between the rich and poor are widening. The wealthy are getting wealthier and adding weight to the burden of poverty that so many are forced to endure. This is not the resource reality that God intends for creation. "Don't be fooled. We're not living in a time of insufficiency," Rev. Dr. Liz Theoharis, co-chair of the Poor People's Campaign, wrote in *The Nation* in February 2023. This is "a golden age of plenty amid grotesque poverty, of abundance amid unbearable forms of abandonment."

Does this mean that we are called to give away everything and live in poverty? Or stop finding joy in the things we have? No. But it does mean that we do not hoard, that we do not build up wealth that oppresses others, and that we do not hold onto things God is calling us to give to the well-being of others.

Jesus's life, death, and resurrection were acts of generosity that push us to reimagine abundance, scarcity, and what is enough. I choose to believe that God is a generous God. And I believe we can become generous too.

What do I have to give?

With a posture of plenty, wisdom, and faith I offer back to God.
   What I have is not mine to store up and hoard.
   What I do is not meant for acknowledgment and affirmation.
   What I believe is not meant to remain stagnant and stale.

What I have, what I do, what I believe come from God,
   with a spirit of hopeful joy,
   with a posture of abundant generosity,
   with trust in God that the world would deny.

I return all that I am and all that I have to God.
   Time. Talent. Treasure.
   Energy. Expertise. Wealth.
   Presence. Passion. Privilege.

I choose generosity because God has been generous to me.

People often wonder, "What do I have to give?" We all have gifts, talents, and resources that God calls us to tend and faithfully steward. We can decide what and how much to give with creativity, generosity, and without resentment. While we offer a blend of gifts back to God, for some it is a portion of our income; for others it's our time; for others it's our expertise and service. Some folks have grown up with the biblical idea that tithing—giving 10 percent of all that you harvest to God—gets us to the ideal amount. Not surprisingly, I am not a big subscriber to rules that could be used to measure faithfulness; then again, the tithe can serve as at least a reminder that we should think intentionally about the amount of our giving relative to our spending and saving. At the end of the day, most of us have more than enough, and we can afford to give some of that back to God, so that work can be done that we cannot do ourselves. So give more money than the scarcity gremlins are telling you that you can afford.

In the same way, don't keep gifts of heart and mind and particular talents and trades under the metaphorical bushel, hoarding them for yourself. Along with financial resources of wealth, offer your talents back to the service of God. Generosity is not solely about money but also about our time and energy. While avoiding workaholism and burnout, we also need to give out of the talents that God has given us. In a world of toxic productivity, grind culture, and worth measured by deliverables, the giving of talents and expertise is one way for us to participate in a different kind of economy. We can participate in and support an economy of generosity and giving—one not measured by the size and trajectory of financial portfolios but by increased healing, thriving, and sufficiency for all.

It is important that giving is not done as an obligatory, resentment-laden sacrifice, as a transactional hedging of an eternal life bet, or as a way of gaining accolades, prestige, or a fancy plaque on the wall. We give because we are grateful, and because it brings us joy to give.

We give not with an expectation of gaining power or influence or say. We give purely because we are grateful for the gifts that God has given us. We know that these gifts are God's, and we are simply returning them to God in order for them to be used in better ways than we could use them ourselves.

REFLECT

Individual: What are the main motivations for you to give of your resources?

Communal: How does your community approach giving?

Practical: For the next day, month, year, and lifetime, how much money would be "enough"?

Montage: What are a few beliefs you have about giving and generosity?

BREATHE

Inhale: "God, what I have,"
Exhale: "Is yours, not mine."

Fourteen

Renewed

A few years after I crashed and burned at my first pastor job, I was called to plant a new church in San Francisco. During the next fourteen years, we created a wonderful, thriving church community. We were young in age, urban in sensibilities, progressive theologically and politically, self-sufficient financially, and committed to the denomination that started us, the Presbyterian Church (USA). I am proud of that work, for sure. But what brings me the most joy is that we were a place where people experienced belonging, were challenged to serve others, and were renewed in body, mind, and spirit.

I will never forget the night Jin came in for a meeting of our leadership council. As a twentysomething, Jin would have been forgiven for thinking that a church committee meeting was not the most exciting way to spend his evening. But Jin came, burrito and beer in hand, plopped himself on the couch, and exhaled, in all seriousness, "I am so glad to be at this meeting!"

While I'd love to believe that his excitement was due to my stunning moderating skills or the inspiring agenda before us, this was not the case. From the get-go, we had decided to center our meetings around food and connection with God and with each other. We viewed meetings as a time of coming to a table prepared by God to eat, meet, and discern together. Our meetings were not solely about tasks and deliverables; they were also about being nurtured and growing in faith. Rather than seeing committee meetings as burdens that drew more energy than they gave, we saw them as gatherings of God's people and as times to be nurtured and renewed.

Like Jin, we can regularly experience the respite and renewal that God provides. When we show up at church meetings or participate in worship services and other rituals, we find sanctuary from the world's constant barrage of expectations, pressures, and demands. Rituals like baptism and communion—outward expressions of our internal connections to God—are especially vital rituals of our faith. They give us a glimpse into God's presence with us in ways that we might not otherwise experience.

Baptism and communion, and any rituals that happen in the church, are not just about the words or going through the motions. These actions ritualize a deep understanding of who God is and how God connects to every one of us in a different way. Sacraments speak to our souls and to the very nature of who we are as Christ-created beings. They speak to the ultimate things of God—sacred truths that defy human understanding and define how we are to be in a relationship with God and with one another. Rituals renew our spirits and nurture our relationship with the divine.

What are sacraments?

As we go, we join with other seeking and searching souls,
    we name, we seal, and we proclaim our commitment to the
        faith.

We claim the faith that we choose to believe
  in ritual and rite,
   sacred and sacramental,
   proclaimed and public,
   jubilant and free.

Something happens in moments of ritual—something invisible and surprising and beyond our ability to articulate. We are given a gift greater than we could ever deserve, and we experience the knowledge and presence of God.

As we craft our communal life, it is important to create space for certain rituals, like baptism and communion, to be lifted up as sacred, as holy, as sacramental. Sacraments differ, depending on your faith tradition. The "rules" for how sacraments are administered, who is allowed to officiate, and who can partake of the sacrament will differ from tradition to tradition. The exact definition of what a sacrament is also varies. Sometimes people get testy when they talk about what constitutes a sacrament and what makes it sacred. Who can blame them? Sacraments are a significant way that we speak to God and God speaks to us. Mess with that, and you might be messing with my relationship with God!

A good general definition of a sacrament is this: an act that has been instituted or enacted by God in the past and that we commit to expressing today. In the Catholic Church, there are seven sacraments: baptism, Holy Communion, confirmation, marriage, ordination, anointing of the sick, and last rites. In most Protestant traditions, like mine, there are just two: baptism and communion, sometimes known as the Eucharist or Lord's Supper.

Both baptism and communion were instituted by Jesus, and they are signs that God is present on earth. As gatherers who worship

God and are called together around the person known as Jesus, we see rituals as a sign of God's presence and an outward expression of an inward commitment. Baptism, which we look at in this chapter, is a way to communally acknowledge that God has claimed us as God's own. Communion, which we'll look at in the next chapter, is the outward and communal expression of remembering that we are one in Christ and that Christ lived, died, and was resurrected for humanity.

What is baptism, and what does it do?

In baptism we are RENEWED.
Renewed, refreshed, and reminded by the water of life,
the flowing waters of our ancestors
the living water of future generations.

Let me begin by saying that being baptized is not a requirement to be seen, known, or loved by God. As with every theological thing we discuss in this book, baptism evokes different understandings, opinions, and experiences. Folks differ on how to celebrate baptism, who to baptize, what baptism means—and yes, whether it is necessary at all. I am not attempting to convince anyone that baptism is an ultimate destination of faith or a way to earn some kind of points. Rather, I hope this explanation of the nature of baptism is helpful for folks who are discerning its value for themselves or the communities of which they are a part.

Full disclosure: I was baptized as an infant, and I have had the honor of baptizing each of my three children. Over the past three decades I have sprinkled water over squirming, crying, and sleeping babies; I have poured water over giggling toddlers; and I have fully immersed grown humans in bodies of water. So yeah, I love me some baptisms.

When I baptize children, the act of a community committing to raise that child feels powerful and spirit-shaking. When I baptize adults, the commitment to seeing the world through a new lens is inspiring and transforming. In baptism, we are claimed and named. Baptism is the tender act of a community saying to a child or an adult that they are special and that they belong: not in a "better than other people" kind of way but a "beyond anything we could ever imagine" kind of belonging.

Being baptized means publicly claiming our place with the cloud of witnesses and the body of Christ. Again, baptism is not a ticket into these communities. But the reciprocal and public nature of the ritual challenges the individual and community to hold one another with loving accountability and committed encouragement. When an adult is baptized, a community of faith says, "You have now made the decision to declare that you are part of this body called together by Christ." When an infant is baptized, the community says, "Those who have made the decision on your behalf have brought you into this body called together by Christ." In both cases, through baptism we are connected to one another beyond our earthly understandings and joined together with our ancestors, those present with us now, and those to come for eternity.

Baptism is made complete by the use of water. Water gives life, cleanses, refreshes, and renews. The same goes for the water of our baptism: in using water that is blessed by God, we are reminded that our lives come from God. Water cleanses us from past choices that held us back from God, and water renews us for the future. The water of baptism is not a "get-out-of-sin-free card," but a way to say publicly that we commit (or commit on behalf of a child) to a new life moving forward. Again: one does not need to be baptized to make these commitments, but baptism operates as a public ritual and reminder that we belong to God.

Ultimately, baptism reminds us that we are not on this journey alone. Through baptism we vow that in the body of Christ—local and global—we will do this thing called faith together.

Is baptism a requirement for salvation, and does it change us?

Baptized not as a transactional act that purchases God's favor, but as a response to what God is doing in our lives and the world.

Christians in some traditions believe baptism is a requirement for salvation: that you must do this act to be welcomed into any kind of eternal relationship with God. This is not only a Catholic belief but one that many Christians hold: that baptism somehow gets a person closer to God.

Many of us, however, view baptism as a personal and communal decision: a way to publicly state that you have a relationship with God and the church that is different now than it was before baptism. There is no special access to the community given, no secrets that can now be shared. In no way does God love someone more or less based on their baptismal status.

Baptism is simply a response to and recognition of a relationship already promised by God. It's a calling to enter a new way of being in a relationship with God, not a guarantee for any kind of exchange with God. Baptism is not transactional. It is an expression of our commitment to God and the community of faith, and it's an acknowledgment of God's commitment to us.

How does baptism impact our lives, and how and when are baptisms done?

Baptized not to settle for a future bound by scarcity,
  but to see dreams realized that are fueled by the abundance
  of God.
Baptized not as a private gesture to prove our purity
of faith,
  but as a public act to proclaim our devotion to one
  another.

The water of baptism washes away that which we thought to be true. Through baptism we declare our commitment to a different set of guiding principles and values. Baptism, taken seriously, changes not only what we do but why we do what we do in the first place. For some, baptism is an invitation to a daily spiritual discipline; for others, it is a recommitment to regular participation in the life of the church. For all of us, this reciprocal commitment between Creator and created should compel us to move through the world in a different way.

In baptism, we no longer see ourselves as individual human beings, simply trying to survive from one paycheck or meal to another. In baptism we acknowledge that we are now accountable to one another—not simply to the communities that we know but to the entirety of God's creation.

Different traditions understand baptism differently in the hows, whos, and whys of the ritual. While much can be debated, I and many others from other traditions maintain two things: that baptism is a public act, and that once baptized, always baptized.

First, while exceptional circumstances may call for private baptism, baptism remains a public ritual. In baptism, we are making a public profession that we are committing our lives to a relationship with God, and a community is vowing to help us grow in that relationship. With these things in mind, it is essential, although not mandatory, that baptism be done in public.

I believe the baptism done by a community of faith is baptism enough and that you do not need to be rebaptized if you join a different community. If you were baptized as an infant, you do not need to be rebaptized. If you were baptized as a Catholic, Protestant, or Orthodox Christian and are now a Pentecostal, Methodist, or nondenominational Christian, you do not need to be rebaptized. Once you have claimed God and God has claimed you, that doesn't change.

Baptisms can be done in a variety of ways, using a variety of words, and none is better or worse than the other. Baptism can be done for infants, with parents making commitments on behalf of a child, or for adults, with the individual making those commitments. And baptisms are enacted in different ways: with the sprinkling of water by hand, the pouring of water with a shell, or with full immersion in a pool, lake, or human-sized feeding trough (sometimes you use what you got).

At the end of the day, whatever the ways or words, the constant is water. Water is water is water: a blessing and a symbol for the unearned gift of being renewed, refreshed, and claimed by God.

Why do we remember our baptisms?

Baptized not as a final destination on our journey to know God,
    but as a commitment to return over and over again to the
    place
where the waterfalls, rivers, and streams of living water flow
unrestrained.

So baptism does not provide access to any aspects of faith that are not accessible to anyone else. Baptism is simply a new commitment to a way of life marked by the public act. That said, rituals and rites of passage mark certain milestones in our lives and are good reminders of past commitments made.

In many traditional church settings, we remember the baptism of Jesus around the beginning of the year. That becomes a time to remember your own baptism. If you were baptized as an infant, you obviously do not literally remember your own baptism, so marking that event becomes an important part of knowing your spiritual path. If you were an adult at your baptism, remembering the time is important, too: to remind yourself of the way you viewed the world before and then after your baptism.

If you take anything away from this baptism chapter, let it be this: Baptism earns you no special treatment from God. Baptism is a public ritual, one that audaciously claims that we rise out of the waters a new creation, and that we are compelled to live as if Christ matters.

REFLECT

Individual: What has been your personal experience of baptism?

Communal: How has your community, family, or church experienced baptism?

Practical: If you have witnessed a baptism, what did you notice?

Montage: What are a few things that you believe about baptism?

BREATHE

Inhale: "God, you know me,"

Exhale: "And you renew me."

Fifteen

Fed

Every Lunar New Year my family would gather around the table. Imagine you are there: The table is filled with food, prepared lovingly by my grandfather and grandmother over the previous few days. There is a hustle and bustle as we find our seats, fighting for positions near our favorite dishes. We ooh and ahh over the spread. The colors and fragrances soothe the soul and bring back memories of past family dinners around that very same table. And then there is the moment when Grandma or Grandpa says something. Perhaps they share a memory from their childhoods, or talk about their future plans, or inquire about the life of one of us around the table. The chit-chat ceases, and the room quiets down. Somehow the meal is transformed from just another family dinner to one that brings in the lessons, struggles, and hopes of our ancestors. This table holds the dreams and disappointments of all of us, and it welcomes in the fullness and messiness of each of our lives. For a moment, family squabbles and resentments are set aside, and we are one.

This memory of my grandparents' table represents, for me, what communion is: a moment in time when we are all—and I mean *all*—welcomed and held at the table. Communion is a time prepared for us by God.

The breaking of the bread and the sharing of the cup take many forms. Throughout history, people have died in debates over the practical application and theological truths concerning communion. Some traditions believe that in the mystery of God, Jesus *is* the actual bread and wine. In those traditions, the bread and the wine are holy in themselves. Others say the bread is not the actual body of Jesus and the cup is not his actual blood but, rather, in the sharing of the bread and the cup, the spirit of Christ is present and made alive again.

At the end of the day, despite its connection to the death of Jesus, communion is a joyous feast. It is a celebration of a people gathered, of a people nourished, and a people promised hope in the future. While at times communion may need to take a more measured tone, most of the time the feast should be celebrated with energy, imagination, and joy. Ultimately, in communion, we're reminded that we are on this journey together. We remember that, no matter how difficult, frustrating, or tiresome the path may become, God nourishes us in body, mind, and soul.

What's so special about the table and who is welcome?

At the communion table, we are FED.
   A table with space for stranger, sibling, sinner, and saint,
   a table set with intention, tenderness, and care,
   a table filled with an overflowing feast of love.
An ever-expanding table for all who wish to take their place.

In the sharing of communion, something special occurs. Yes, it is just a table, metaphorical or physical, but it is sacred, because Christ invites us into a relationship that is not bound by the limitations of human understanding of community. The table is a place to which we are invited to unapologetically bring our whole selves: our culture, contexts, loves, hates, joys, sorrows, struggles, and celebrations. In communion, we hold one another with the love that God offers us. We are given permission to let go of all the analyses, assessments, and judgments that we bring to most interactions. Communion calls us to be vulnerable, open, and willing to see one another as the beautifully created human beings that we are. There are very few places where we can experience this reality. The communion table is the place we come to closest to seeing one another with the purity and love with which God sees us every day.

Who is welcome at the table varies from congregation to congregation. Some traditions require that you be baptized or affirm a set of beliefs in order to receive communion. I believe the most welcoming table is one that invites all people. So while some churches' rules regulate who is allowed to receive communion, I and many others believe the table is open to everyone. The last thing the world needs is more barriers to relationships, walls that increase separation, and borders that divide faith. (Note: Welcome also means having integrity and clarity about when and how we welcome perpetrators and victims to a common table.) The table is one of the few places where we are invited to bring our entire selves and to honor the fullness of those seated with us.

If we believe that God's open table expands our connection with other human beings, then we are compelled to open the table up to as many people as possible and share this amazing gift. When God calls together God's beloved people, it is a place genuinely and truly open to all.

What is significant about the bread?

Here our hunger is nourished by the bread of life,
  the bread blessed and broken.

For many years, my children did not believe that communion was *real* unless the church was using Hawaiian bread and grape juice. Those were the communion elements our church used. Kids can be rigid—and I remind them of this when they tease *me* for being old and set in my ways.

In many traditions, we understand communion bread to be the bread of the people. So, depending upon your context, the ritual bread could be a variety of things: tortillas, sourdough bread, steamed bao, even goldfish crackers. The key is that the bread represents Jesus's body and that it reminds us that we are the body of Christ together.

When we come to the table, we remember that Jesus lived and died and was resurrected. His body was broken for us. The crucifixion is the culmination of so much of his life. Jesus was brought to the cross by institutions and powers that were threatened by his words and actions. Jesus was broken and mocked by those who had earlier been cheering him on. Jesus tells us again and again that we are all one body, connected to one another, despite our best efforts as humans to be divided from one another. Jesus promises that even when we are suffering and hungry, he will feed and nourish our bodies and spirits. The bread represents an invisible truth: that Christ walked this journey with us, and that even in the face of humanity breaking him, he nourishes us still.

When we come to the communion table, the bread reminds us that Christ is still among us: in death and in life. In the breaking and sharing of the bread, we remember that we are the body of Christ. We suffer together, and we are fed together.

What is significant about the cup?

Here our thirst is quenched by the cup of the new promise,
the cup poured and passed.

The cup is often called the cup of salvation, or the cup of the new promise, or the blood of Christ. Those terms can seem a little bit odd and may even make some feel a little queasy. Drinking blood?

But it's not blood. It has never been blood. It's a symbol. The cup reminds us of what it meant for Jesus to live, die, and be resurrected, and what it means for us now: that there is a new beginning. Jesus said there is a new day coming, and someday we will realize the promise of hope and new life beyond the despair and death. In the pouring and sharing of the cup, we are reminded that there is hope beyond a burning, groaning world.

In that cup, we receive a new promise: that Jesus will come again, in some form, in some way. (Also: not our job to figure out the exact timing or form.) In that promise, we are given hope that someday there will be a new and a better world. The cup of the new promise is about moving from this world into the next. When we drink it, we celebrate the promise that someday Christ will return and usher in a new creation, a new life, and a new way of being.

How shall communion be celebrated?

Here a feast of faith is joyfully shared by the people of God,
  a feast that nourishes and nurtures us all for the journey home.

Communion is an important ritual in many Christian traditions, and congregations celebrate communion in particular ways. Different Christians understand the elements—the bread and the cup—differently. Some believe that the elements themselves are holy, so they should be treated with reverence. In my tradition and many others, communion is less about the bread and cup themselves and more about the spirit of Christ that is present in the feast.

Some communities share one loaf and drink from one cup. Some dip the bread in the wine; other congregations serve them separately. Some use prepackaged and prepared elements, and others only use unleavened bread and wine. I have been to churches that use tortillas and wine and churches that use steamed bao and tea. I do not believe the elements matter as long as they are the bread and cup of the people. We meet Christ in the elements. He makes himself known in both the communion feast and the everyday meals we share.

So the way we take communion is informed by the history and culture and faith tradition in which a community is lodged. No matter the specifics, we can receive the bread and the cup with a new heart, new eyes, and a new understanding that it is not just any meal. Communion is a spiritual feast, so no matter how we may receive it, it is a symbol, a statement, and a communal acknowledgment that we are joined together in the body of Christ. Through the bread and the cup we are nourished. We are reminded, again and again, that God is here.

REFLECT

Individual: What has been your personal experience of communion?

Communal: How does your faith community understand, interpret, and practice communion?

Practical: Describe the last communion you witnessed or participated in and what, if any, questions it raised.

Montage: What are a few things that you believe about communion?

BREATHE

Inhale: "God, you know me,"
Exhale: "And God, you claim me."

Sixteen

A Few Words about the Good News and Us

I mentioned that our eldest child got into trouble at preschool. One more event—what our family calls the Great Circle Time Rebellion of 1999—led to a mutual agreement to part ways with that preschool.

You likely know about circle time, when teachers gather all the children at the beginning of the day. Sometime in the fall, Ev shared with us that they didn't want to stay in circle time. In a genuine attempt to recognize the agency of a child, the teachers agreed to let Ev opt out of circle time and read a book in the reading nook. This arrangement seemed to work out fine for all parties.

Upon the return from holiday break, Ev assumed that the rules would be the same. So when circle time started, Ev got up, grabbed a book, and headed over to the reading nook. I can imagine that some of the new kids, and maybe some of the old-timers too, were wondering, "What's going on? Why does Ev get to skip circle time? I want to do that too." So one by one, kids left circle time and joined Ev. Circle time was ruined.

That afternoon we received a call with another invitation to meet with the principal, Ms. C. This time, however, we were not told a story about Ev being bullied by some other kid. This time we were asked to get our child to "conform" to what the rest of the class was doing. Wrong word, wrong parents. Thus the mutual agreement to part ways.

To be clear, Ev did not intend to start an anti–circle-time movement. Ev was simply moving through the situation as best they knew how and within the bounds of the agreed-upon rules—and lo and behold, other people followed.

As Ev did in leading their classmates to a new place, we might find that the most effective way to share our faith—this story of God that we love—is to simply be faithful to God's call. We liberate others by simply living in the liberating truth of God ourselves. When it comes to sharing faith with others, it will take intention, but it will not require using coercive tactics, placing expectations upon relationships, or developing steps or prayers or strategies designed to lead others to some desired and predetermined outcome.

In Matthew 28:19–20, we are offered what is known as the Great Commission: "Therefore go and make disciples of all nations, baptizing them in the name of the Father and of the Son and of the Holy Spirit, and teaching them to obey everything I have commanded you. And surely I am with you always, to the very end of the age." This is often understood as a command to go and convert people. Unfortunately, this posture has created an arrogance about our own faith that treats others as objects, that makes us feel like they are just one good explanation or mission effort away from choosing Christianity. Everyone must be told about Jesus, we begin to think, because Jesus *commanded* us to tell everyone in the world about him! The mere mention of the word *evangelism* sends shivers down the spines of so many.

Thankfully, those who remember and understand their Greek participles far better than I do have translated this passage not as an urgent command to go and make disciples but as a comforting reminder that "as you go," or "whenever you go," go and make disciples. This tone invites us into a more relational posture of sharing. We are still called to share, just with humility, awareness, empathy, and care.

As we unpack this idea of evangelism, we will look at some examples about how we are called to go. I will end this book with an invitation to think about how you will share as you go. This is not a command. Our calling to share our faith is not a transaction or even an expectation. It is a response to what God has done in our lives. I will invite you to navigate the world with the same expansiveness, openness, compassion, patience, and hopefulness that God offers us.

What do we do with the word *evangelism*?

As we are sent, as we are called, as we choose to go into the world
  the body of Christ,
  dwelling amidst the body politic,
  seeking the common good for all.

Evangelism is dead to me. Okay, not the idea but the word. As a card-carrying liberal Christian, I have spent far too much time and energy trying to wrestle the word back from those who have turned it into colonization, saviorism, and "we know better than you, so we're going to tell you how you should live"-ism. While I send no shade to colleagues who are still trying to redefine and reclaim and rehabilitate evangelism, I am done. Take it. You can have it. I'm done.

Again, though: I'm done with the *word*, not the *action*.

Some say the same thing about *good news* and *gospel*. Both are very churchy words, grounded in the announcement of victory over one's enemy! Obviously I am holding onto these two for now. We all find the words that work for us, as well as the ones that don't.

If it's not clear yet, I believe that there is a much better version of the gospel to be shared. And I believe we can share the good news in a way that is not oppressive, condescending, or patronizing. The faith I have described in the pages of this book, should you find it compelling and shareable, invites people into a conversation, listens without judgment, welcomes disagreement, honors nuance, reciprocates openness, and measures maturity on the depth of engagement, not arrival at doctrinal purity or agreement with a particular creed. Sharing our faith should not be driven by the need to get someone to make a particular commitment. Don't get me wrong: when I've shared my faith with someone else and they've chosen to become a Christian, I have been thrilled. The sharing of our faith is about sharing a particular story of transformation, love, and belonging. If people hear that story, are drawn to it, and begin to inquire more deeply, great! If they don't—if they choose another spiritual path or no faith at all—well, that's fine too. Remember, the version of the gospel that I hope I am sharing does not claim that Jesus is the only way to connect to God. It is the way I choose to connect to God, but I do not believe that it is the only way. I do not feel the urgency to convince everyone that I meet that they better hurry up and meet Jesus before it's too late.

I am so grateful for those who have shared—and still share—their faith with me. "Sharing your faith" isn't a once-and-done thing, and it's not a one-way street directed at non-Christians. Other Christians still share their faith with me: they encourage me to seek growth in faith and connection to God. Knowing that there is no pressure makes the things I do believe that much more meaningful.

So go ahead and remove the word *evangelism* from your lexicon of faith if you need to. But do not shy away from the call and command to share the faith as you go. If you hear a good story, and if that story gives you a deep sense of being loved by God, you will likely want to share it with others.

The next few chapters will offer reflections on the sharing of faith. Truth be told, this is where I get most excited about faith. My own faith journey, and the ways that I have seen faith impact the world for good, compel me to share the faith. Our "tactics" for sharing the faith must reflect the *character* of the faith that we are attempting to share and I hope these chapters will help you share in a way that reflects the very faith that you choose to follow.

REFLECT

Individual: How have you understood evangelism?

Communal: How does your faith community understand, interpret, and practice evangelism?

Practical: What is one way that you could share your faith with a colleague, friend, or stranger?

Montage: What are a few beliefs you have about evangelism?

BREATHE

Inhale: "As I go,"

Exhale: "I will share love."

Seventeen

Humble

When I was in seminary, I was often invited to be a guest preacher at local congregations. At one of them I learned a great lesson in humility.

I was guest preaching one particular Sunday and, wow, was I good! When I was done preaching, I was feeling myself. I preached the gospel hard. In fact, I was pretty sure that if I *hadn't* preached that masterpiece of a sermon, Jesus might not have shown up that day. I mean, thank God for me.

At the completion of the worship service, as is tradition, I stood at the back of the sanctuary to greet people as they left. I stood there, ready to receive all the exuberant accolades. And as people filed out and affirmed the sermon, like the humble servant that I was, I believed every single doggone word. Yes, I was insufferable.

As the congregation thinned and the line slowed down, I checked my watch, ready to get on with the rest of my day. My stomach was grumbling and I was eager for lunch, but a little old lady had different plans for me. Keep in mind that, at 5'5", I can call very few people "little," so normally I am very patient with those of us who take short strides. Not today. I got impatient as I saw her strolling slowly down the aisle, taking her little old lady time. I mentally begged her to hurry, as I had places to go and things to eat. Couldn't she just please hurry up, tell me what an amazing, inspiring, and Spirit-filled sermon I had just preached, and let us both get on with our day?

When she finally arrived, she grabbed my hand in hers, looked up at me, and said, without a hint of irony, sarcasm, or meanness, "My, what a big voice for such a little man!"

Then off she went, sauntering into the afternoon sun, like the church lady gangster that she was. Much respect, little old lady. Much respect.

Years later, I carry her with me wherever I go. Too often we fall into the trap of believing we are God. We are not. I carry the story with me because it's easy to forget that all that I am, and all that I do, comes from God.

In our eagerness to choose faith, we could easily begin to believe that everything *we* think about God is always true. Yes, I have gifts and talents that have been helpful and healing to some. You do too. Yet these things do not come solely from our own efforts. Every breath that I breathe comes from God; the Spirit is the one who sweeps through my heart and mind to inspire and prod; and Jesus models the complexities of living with intention and faith. Given these truths, I have no choice but to be humble. God has been generous, and we must submit to that reality. It is God who has given us life, both ephemeral and enduring. Thank God that we do not know everything. Our lives are made fuller both by knowing God and by knowing we don't have all the answers.

What is humility?

We go with minds and hearts that are HUMBLE
*   to share a faith strengthened by always seeking God.*

Humility is central to Jesus's identity as Priest. (Remember the fourfold nature of Jesus?) One must be humble to appreciate the spiritual disciplines and the ongoing need to learn, grow, study, and reflect. Jesus the Priest reminds me that I do not have to invent or discover everything on my own; in fact, I should very much not invent my own way. Instead, I should be humble enough to know that truth, answers, and growth will come only through a committed life of seeking God's will. This seeking will take many forms: reading, study, rest, prayer, worship, discomfort, sorrow, joy, and celebration. Resting in the knowledge that I do not always have to know the answer gives me permission to be humble in what I *think* I believe, what beliefs I share, and how I share them.

Why choose humility?

If you're looking for the short answer about why to be humble, here it is: God, through Scripture, tells us over and over again to be humble. A central Scripture passage that will run through these last few chapters is Micah 6:8. The passage occurs just after God has lamented the fact that humanity seems to keep forgetting how to act. I can almost hear the frustration and exasperation in God's voice: "He has told you, human one, what is good and what the Lord requires from you: to do justice, embrace faithful love, and walk humbly with your God."

Being humble doesn't mean holding a negative sense about who we are. It *does* mean that we do not put ourselves in the place of God. When we lose humility, we begin to believe we are the center of all that happens. We have the answers that all should know, and we move into a colonial mindset about faith that not only turns people off but is also wrong. To be humble is to remember that God is God and we are humans. Yes, we can accomplish amazing things, but we do so because God has provided ancestors and saints to pave the way.

God has called us and nurtured us into situations where we grow, and God is with us when we struggle and when we celebrate. God calls us into being more than we could imagine, yes. But that calling should give us not an arrogance of faith but a wellspring of humility.

What does lived humility look like?

Spirit-led humility means knowing when to be vulnerable and when to be forthright. Humility in sharing your faith means understanding your surroundings and knowing how, when, and if to talk about faith.

Lived humility, when sharing faith, means that your primary intent in any interaction is to learn to know someone, absent any strategy or timeline. There is no assumed or hoped-for outcome other than a genuine interest in the well-being of the other person. In this model of "sharing the good news," as it is sometimes called, you get to simply interact with the human across from you. We release ourselves from thinking that we know the ideal ending, and we open ourselves up to the possibilities that may be revealed for all involved. And in that, the open, loving, and humble faith that we hope to share is, in fact, shared.

So the next time you are out loving life—whether it's in a grocery store or a café or the pick-up line at school—be open to the faith-sharing opportunities that may present themselves. I'm not saying that you should lead off with conversations about faith; leave room to simply get to know the humans around you. Share the story of God that you know and have experienced. Do it not because you're afraid the other person will go to hell if you don't, or to convert them to your religion, or to show them how you're right and they're wrong. Rather, tell a story of faith that claims that what is good about God—love, kindness, justice, belonging, openness, goodness, truth, healing—is actually, simply, wonderfully, true.

REFLECT

Individual: What person in your life exemplifies the best of what it means to be humble?

Communal: In what areas or practices does your community most exemplify what it means to be humble?

Practical: What is one practice and area where you express the best of what it means to be humble?

Montage: What do you believe about humility?

BREATHE

Inhale: "God, grant me the capacity,"
Exhale: "To be humble."

Eighteen

Just

I mentioned the preaching class that I took in seminary from the Rev. Dr. J. Alfred Smith. In that story, I avoided being the one called up to the front to preach a spontaneous sermon, on a Scripture text that had just been given. But my luck did not last.

When it was my turn to come up to the front of the class and preach off the cuff, I walked up with bravery and confidence. (It was more like with sweaty palms and terror.) I don't remember exactly which passage Dr. Smith read to me, but I do remember that it was about the plight of the poor and the burden of economic injustice.

I had no words. I just stood there. He read the passage again. I still had no words. I still just stood there.

Finally he asked, "So what's going on?"

"I can't speak to this," I mumbled. "This level of poverty and oppression is not my experience."

He gently and firmly reminded me that preaching about any injustice did not require me to have personally experienced all kinds of injustice. He impressed upon me that, out of the context of my privilege and influence, I was convicted, called, and compelled to engage in the cause for justice. Yes, we need to be careful when and how we talk about situations that we have not known personally, and we need to be aware of the space we take in conversations. But at the end of the day, God calls us all to live lives of justice. In fact, to refuse this command may often lead to the perpetuation of the injustice that we claim to stand against. Remember Micah 6:8? "He has told you, human one, what is good and what the Lord requires from you: to do justice, embrace faithful love, and walk humbly with your God."

Like most areas of my faith, I look at living a just life through the lens of the fourfold Jesus: Prophet, Pastor, Priest, and Poet. The prophetic Jesus once led me to be arrested on the US–Mexico border, along with forty colleagues, as we protested our government's treatment of migrants. The pastoral Jesus led me to participate in an accompaniment program that helped to settle and support a trans asylum seeker from Honduras. The priestly Jesus has led me to preach sermons, create worship liturgies, and write prayers that build a deeper understanding of experiences such as gender fluidity, poverty, gun violence, and reproductive rights. And the creative Jesus has led me to embrace social media and digital communication as a way to share faith through word and image.

Let's be clear: Jesus did much of his ministry by fighting institutions of power, religious and political, while also encouraging his followers to take part in the life of civil society. From questioning religious leaders (who thought he could not heal on the Sabbath), to rejecting social norms around gender (talking to a Samaritan woman in public), to challenging ideas around money (storing up grain doesn't mean you'll be able to keep it when you get to heaven), Jesus calls us to challenge institutions and individuals who take advantage of and oppress those who have no power.

Some traditions shy away from even the term *social justice* because it "feels too political." I have never really understood this as a biblical stance, because Jesus was political insofar as he was fully engaged in the body politic. He challenged religious institutions when he questioned their leaders, he rejected cultural norms of the day when he spoke with and healed those who were marginalized by society, and he constantly drew attention to the plight and lifted the burdens of those caught in poverty. He took seriously the idea that we are all part of one body.

So if we take seriously the idea that we are all part of one body, how can we *not* stand against injustice as Jesus did? What if by working for justice, sometimes publicly and politically, we are actually sharing the good news?

What role do we play in creating a just world?

We go with hands and feet that are JUST
  to take part in God's healing of a hurting world

That pesky Jesus, the Prophet, shows up again here. Remember, prophets' work is not about foretelling the future but about telling the *reality* of God to those who may or may not want to believe it. Prophetic witness, when we're calling another person or community to account, can be invigorating. Prophetic witness, when it's directed at *us*, is not as much fun.

Many of us know what it's like to be preached at. We know what it's like to be told that we do not have the truth. We've been made audience to the bullhorn and the billboard. In some ways, the prophetic Jesus might appear similar to those voices. But he is not. Jesus the Prophet knows that to fully know God, we must listen to the voices of those most impacted by injustice. Jesus lived among the oppressed; he *was* the oppressed. He knows that those Howard Thurman said have "their backs against the wall"—the disinherited—belong smack-dab in the middle of the process of seeking a right and just future.

In the struggle for justice, and when it comes to sharing the prophetic nature of Jesus, the potential for saviorism and condescension is ripe. It's important to know when and where we should place ourselves in the struggle. Sometimes it is *our* struggle for justice, so we should be centered and take the space we are entitled to; at other times we are co-conspirators and accomplices, offering any support, resources, and influence that our privilege affords. Together, we work to experience the justice after injustice.

What is justice and why should we choose it?

In one sense, justice refers to prisons, courts, and law enforcement; in another, justice is about making right that which has been unfair or unjust or unequal. That is the justice that I am talking about: the justice that claims and names what is right and good and fair in the eyes of God and then lives and expresses that, as much as is possible. Justice is not just about how we treat one another; it is also about institutional and systemic oppression, the effects of capitalism, and the ways our politics have reinforced institutions and built systems that normalize oppression, exclusion, and marginalization. God helps us to navigate these systems and advocate for solutions: not to build up a theocracy, but to ensure that institutions are taking care of their citizens.

We choose justice because we refuse to allow injustice, oppression, and suffering to have the final word. A commitment to justice can run counter to our commitment to humility. But that is a chance we take in this calling to be prophetic in the world. I hope that you choose a life of justice—and that you do so humbly, publicly, and faithfully.

We choose justice because we take seriously the idea that we are all part of one body. We take notice when part of that body is suffering, as we hear in 1 Corinthians 12:26–27: "If one part suffers, all the parts suffer with it; if one part gets the glory, all the parts celebrate with it. You are the body of Christ and parts of each other."

While hunkering down in our places of comfort and security is easier than following God's call to do justice, if we take our faith seriously, we simply cannot do that. Too many of our siblings, neighbors, strangers, and friends are experiencing oppression, marginalization, and violence in body, mind, and spirit. If we simply pass by as onlookers, we become reinforcers, conspirators, and perpetrators, not of healing and hope but of pain and despair.

What does lived justice look like?

A posture of justice cannot stay in the abstract. We must not intellectualize justice to the point that we talk so much about it that we fool ourselves into thinking we have acted. Justice requires—nay, demands—action. At the risk of this turning into a litmus test list or voting guide, I believe that the faith I hold and advocate for has implications for how I vote, speak, protest, engage, proclaim, support, collaborate, and advocate. You may be able to hazard a guess about how I would land regarding certain social, cultural, and legislative issues. I hope that you, too, will unapologetically use your faith as you develop beliefs and make decisions about how you spend your energy, resources, and influence. Issues like restrictive reproductive rights, gun violence, transphobia, racism, climate change, xenophobia, housing injustice, healthcare inequity, police brutality, and educational apartheid are too important for us not to be involved.

We cannot fully live the faith of Christ if we leave out the clear call to justice. So as you go, be aware of injustice around you. As God leads, seek to right that which is wrong.

REFLECT

Individual: Who in your life exemplifies the best of what it means to be just?

Communal: In what areas or practices does your community most exemplify what it means to be just?

Practical: What is one practice and area where you express the best of what it means to be just?

Montage: What do you believe about justice?

BREATHE

Inhale: "God, grant me the passion,"
Exhale: "To be just."

Nineteen

Kind

I am not kind by nature. I have strong opinions about many things and about people who hold opinions that differ from mine. I have been known to see driving as personal warfare. I do not understand people who are late. I get peeved by a consistent lack of individual preparation that leads to communal emergencies. And don't get me started on the damage pastors and other faith leaders often do. The list is long.

But gosh darn it, if the command to be kind doesn't always show its pesky little face!

Here we go again with the Micah 6:8 passage: "He has told you, human one, what is good and what the Lord requires from you: to do justice, embrace faithful love, and walk humbly with your God." "Embrace faithful love" is often translated as "love kindness."

Kindness—our ability to see the humanity of all people and to act accordingly—is an essential aspect of what humanity needs today. Kindness is power. Kindness is liberation. Kindness of love.

What is kindness?

We go with souls and spirits that are KIND
to tell God's story of dignity, empathy, and love.

In 2021 I wrote a book titled *In Defense of Kindness*. In that book, I wrote that to be kind is "to accept that each person is a created and complex human being—and to treat them as if you believe this to be true." Kindness is a choice, I said, "to honor the humanity (holiness) that lies within each and every one of us."

When Jesus the Pastor steps into the picture, we learn exactly what kindness looks like. The pastoral role of Jesus is to tend to those who have been called into community. This idea comes from an old understanding of a king—that the responsibility of a king is to take care of their people. Similarly, the pastor is to take care of those they have been charged to serve. At the heart of the pastoral Jesus lies an impulse to extend kindness.

Kindness is not about being nice or about avoiding conflict or about making sure we don't rock the boat. Kindness is about seeing others—and ourselves—as complex, unique creations that are always beautiful, often broken, and sometimes living in grief. Kindness means assuming others are more than what you see. Kindness challenges us to embrace the complexities of every situation and every person—yes, both friend and foe.

From stepping away from harmful situations as a kindness to ourselves, to seeing protest through the eyes of those who take to the streets, to remembering, in the school drop-off line, that other parents and kids are facing struggles we don't see, kindness is a choice, one that can infiltrate all aspects of our lives. Kindness is a choice to see others in the way that God sees us.

Why choose kindness—and what does it look like?

While *not* being kind may provide short-term satisfaction (don't ask me how I know), I hope we choose kindness more often than we don't. Put simply, choosing kindness is a better, healthier, more meaningful way to live than choosing vengeance, cruelty, *ad hominem* attacks, or just plain ol' mean-spiritedness. The apostle Paul wrote in Romans 12:21, "Don't be defeated by evil, but defeat evil with good." Choosing kindness means not letting ourselves get defeated by evil.

With the ongoing divisions about politics, ideology, faith, and culture, the easy response—and dare I say the lazy one—is to return the vitriol. Kindness, on the other hand, helps us solve problems and address conflicts. In holding a posture of kindness, we give ourselves the collective opportunity not only to find solutions to the world's problems but also to experience healing between the world's people. Choosing kindness across divisions of politics, ideology, relationships, and experiences gives us permission to put aside perspectives that preserve power at the expense of others. While kindness does not mean that we remain in situations of abuse, trauma, or exploitation, kindness does prompt us to see others as deserving of the same dignity and respect that we hope others would show us. And kindness precipitates individual and social healing that may otherwise seem unattainable.

Let's be clear: to live kindly is excruciating. We do not become kind people overnight. You can't simply get up one morning and say, "I am now antiracist," or "I am not misogynistic," or "I am fully

LGBTQIA+ affirming," or "I now make climate-friendly decisions" and expect all these things to be true. In order to truly *become* these things, we must practice, fail, and practice again. In essence, we must choose every day to live differently than the world would want us to live. Choosing kindness requires the same commitment. Throughout each day and in each interaction, we must commit to seeing and valuing others as the beloved creatures that they are.

Kindness begins with intentionality: with the simple (and difficult) act of noticing. When I arrive at my favorite café, I remind myself to choose kindness. I try to notice people in line, and those who are preparing my drink. In my mind, I acknowledge that they are complex human beings, loved by God, and that they may be dealing with situations. So when somebody seems stressed in line, I simply move out of the way. If a barista seems a little off, I offer a smile and a hello. I don't do these things with an expectation of anything in return but with the hope that a small gesture of kindness might improve their day.

Kindness is an acknowledgment that we are all created beings and that, embodied as one body, we are complex and beautiful. It demands that we see one another fully and notice how we treat one another daily. Exhibiting kindness must not be treated as an intellectual exercise or an afterthought. Kindness is a calling. As we go forth in kindness, we lean into a transformative power, one that might heal humanity in amazing and unexpected ways.

REFLECT

Individual: Who in your life exemplifies the best of what it means to be kind?

Communal: In what areas or practices does your community most exemplify what it means to be kind?

Practical: What is one practice and area where you express the best of what it means to be kind?

Montage: What do you believe about kindness?

BREATHE

Inhale: "God, grant me the courage,"
Exhale: "To be kind."

Twenty

Led

A parishioner in a church I was serving in the San Francisco Bay Area was entering the final stages of life. Fred was receiving hospice care at his home, where his family was also tending to him. It was my duty and my honor, as his pastor, to visit during this time: to share the word of the love that his church offered, to bring him communion, and to pray with him. So I showed up, ready to spend the afternoon with him and his wife.

I had not been serving long at this church, but I already knew that Fred and I stood on different sides of every theological and political spectrum. This was during a time in our national life when debates about politics and theology were especially heated. So when, during our conversation, Fred asked his wife to step out of the room so he could have a few moments with me alone, I was half expecting to receive some last-minute lashing about what I had preached on Sunday. I thought he might chastise me about where the church was headed, or perhaps offer an aggrieved lament over the ills of this fallen world.

To my surprise, Fred began by thanking me for leading the congregation that he so loved. Then, with tears of hope in his eyes, he took his hands in mine and asked me earnestly, "What does God want me to do with the rest of my life?"

I was stunned. This man—who had maybe a few weeks, maybe a few months to live—was still seeking God's leading, even to his final breaths. I sat there in pure awe, the kind of awe that transcends respect or admiration. I am sure that we would like to think that, in the same situation, we would be as faithful. But I wonder if most of us have cultivated such a deep well of faith and trust in God. Until that day, I didn't even know what that well looked like.

I asked Fred some questions to draw out his own discernment of God's will for him. I reminded him that his community loved him, and I thanked him for giving me an example of a faith built on an openness to what God may reveal.

I am as guilty as anyone of being driven by what I want to do and where I want to go rather than by what God intends for me to do and where God intends me to go. Like so many who have been taught that overwork and workaholism are badges of honor, I have spent far too long swimming in the waters of toxic productivity, grind culture, and exploitative capitalism. In that short interaction with Fred, I found that the illusion of a successful life—that well-curated version of career, ambition, and productivity—was shattered. A purposeful life, one that is well-lived and meaningful, is a life shaped by the question that Fred was asking.

In asking that singular question, "What does God want me to do with the rest of my life?" Fred showed me that even to the end of our days, our worth comes from following God's lead, not the world's.

What does it mean to be led by God?

And we go LED by the God who sends us, calls us back, and sends us again
    to be and become more than we could ever dream for ourselves.

The last element of how we share the story as we go is being led by the Spirit: the creative, artistic, adventurous, poetic Spirit. It is in this vein that Jesus the Poet joins us, with sweeping and audacious brushstrokes of possibility. Poet Jesus comes in to inspire and compel and convict us to be better in the world. He helps us to imagine the unimaginable and then to move toward that reality.

This perspective on life is contagious. This posture helps us move beyond and above hatred and violence; it also gives people hope for actual love and healing. When we risk being open to a new way of being, God can produce something more beautiful than what we can fathom.

Why choose to be led by God?

As I have gotten older and less interested in chasing positions of prestige or roles of influence, I have become more open than ever to creative possibilities. Frankly, I'm now willing and able to try just about anything. As I age, I don't want to get more conservative or calcified or driven by a need to pad my retirement account or rack up lifetime achievement awards. Rather, I long to follow Poet Jesus. Like Fred of the "What does God want me to do?" interaction, I want to follow God to the end of my days. Central to that following is to claim, over and over again, my choice to participate in the reimagining of the world. I want to be a collaborator with God, and I want to bring to fruition here on earth harmony, joy, hope, and love. I want to be led by God.

The world offers a seemingly nonstop barrage of pain and suffering. So as I go, I want to exhibit a faith that proclaims endless possibilities of healing and hope. I believe that God calls us to be creative in how we participate in movements that produce long-term, deep, and meaningful change. Placing trust in God's leading, we allow ourselves to see the boundless energy and imagination possible. We free ourselves up from looking for human affirmation and believe instead that our worth comes from truly following the lead of God.

What does a life led by God look like?

Being led by a creative God means that we do not let ourselves be defined solely by our work or the things we own. While we all participate in economies of some kind, we should not remain loyal to them when they treat workers as merely a means to profit. Instead, a creative God challenges us to be loyal to and follow a God who sees the wholeness of the workers (us). A creative God emboldens us to live with faithful intention, and work is a part of that intention; this perspective is different from living as if working is our primary purpose. And while some organizations and companies may be doing good in the world, ultimately, our worth does not come from those particular things but from following God.

Being led by this creative God means investing time, energy, and resources into organizations and activities that bring you joy, regardless of the economies to which you may be tied. Being led by this creative God means that no matter what job you have or how little money you make, you find ways to participate in the future that God is revealing. You take time to nurture and cultivate creativity that is given life in your passions and commitments. You claim liberation from what the world wants you to do and find creative ways to do what God hopes for you to do.

You are tired of asking the same old questions, the questions we are taught to ask: How can I make more money? How can I make sure my family and I are safe and comfortable? How can we have more thrills and more fun? How can I be happy?

You know there are better questions to ask, and so you are choosing a faith that helps you ask them. How is God present with us? How does the Spirit move? Who was Jesus—and who am I? How can I be part of God's story? What rituals connect me to God and the community? How can I live more humbly, justly, and kindly? What does God want me to do with the rest of my life? And what if everything good about God is actually true?

REFLECT

> *Individual:* Who in your life exemplifies the best of what it means to be led by God?
>
> *Communal:* In what areas or practices does your community most exemplify what it means to be led by God?
>
> *Practical:* What is one practice and area where you express the best of what it means to be led by God?
>
> *Montage:* What do you believe about being led by God?

BREATHE

> *Inhale:* "God, grant me the wisdom,"
> *Exhale:* "To be led by you."

Epilogue

Many times during the writing of this theological monstrosity of love, I wanted to give up. I mean, what had I been thinking? With every chapter and every draft, the whole project—trying to communicate my understanding of Christianity—seemed more audacious and more absurd. My sense of inadequacy grew, like some childhood monster lurking just behind the closet door.

And then, after my editor would talk me off the cliff, I'd read what I had written; talk through ideas with myself, my plants, and the occasional human; and challenge myself to return to the premise of this entire endeavor. The premise is this: I believe in a faith that is not all that complex or complicated, and I trust in a God whose goodness is entirely true. I hope that I have articulated this simple faith, this good God, in a way that you, my reader, find compelling.

In many ways I end where I began: embracing the pure, simple, faithful approach to life that Bishop Desmond Tutu modeled for me while standing in that inaugural procession line. Stripped of regalia and presumptions, we are all just humans being humans. We're all just standing around in line together, trying to be faithful to God.

So if you are one of those people who reads the epilogue first, I am risking spoiling the entire book for you. If you take one sentiment from this book, I hope it is this:

You are known by God.
You are loved by God.
That is enough.
You are enough.

If you've read the whole thing and are absorbing all that we've discussed, I hope you now explore your own faith, your relationship with God, and your connection to communities of humans around you. Most importantly, I hope that something that I have offered will encourage, compel, and call you to make the world a better place as you go.

I offer one final prayer in the form of a charge and benediction. I have been using this benediction in various forms since I was ordained almost thirty years ago. It is a mishmash of words I've heard and thoughts I've had over the years, and I use it at every service that I officiate or lead.

Go forth into the world with compassion and justice in your heart
Hear voices of the long-silenced
See strength in that which has been deemed weak
See one another
Hear one another
Care for one another
And love one another
It's all that easy
And it's all that hard

Now may the grace of God
The love of Christ
And the power of the Holy Spirit
Be with us all, now and forevermore
And all God's people say—Amen.

God knows you.
God loves you.
That is enough.
Go in peace.

My Faith Montage

offer my own faith montage as a prompt for you to craft your own. I will also be crafting liturgies and prayers using this faith montage, so be sure to keep up with me via @breyeschow on all the social platforms. I am always humbled and excited when folks find my work worthy of use, so you are invited to use this montage and any future liturgy in your context. If you do, I only ask for attribution when possible. Other than that, I offer these words to the community and hope that they collectively move us a little more toward love.

I choose to believe that, in life and in death, I belong to God.
God stirs my soul.
In the morning, life-giving first breath fills my lungs.
God stills my spirit.
In the evening, the calm of the night flows through my body.
God moves me.
The Holy One beckons me forth, through bands of light, into coves of darkness,
woven into rainbows, and amid the in-between and unknown—
All the while, with every tender breath,
I am reminded of God's hoping, yearning, and dreaming that I grow into all I am intended to become.

I am **GROUNDED** in the presence of God.
>God knows me.
>God sees me.
>God loves me.
>And that is enough.

>God is with me.
>God has been with me.
>God will always be with me.

Through crawling minutes and blurred decades,
mundane whispers and shouts of magnificence,
awkward encounters and an impassioned embrace,
brisk breezes, warm skies, cool fog, living deserts, flourishing
>forests, living water,
the farm, the field, the town, the suburb, the streets, and the
>city,

during protests, parties, feasts, and funerals,
at coffee shops, clubs, stages, pitches, courts, corners, class-
>rooms, playgrounds, porches,
barbershops, dining tables, couches, screens, and every unex-
>pected holy space:

Through and in it all, God is known to my soul,
>and I am reminded that I am known by God.

Created in the image of God,
I choose to join with others as God's **GATHERED**.

We are the body gathered,
beautiful, powerful, holy bodies.

These bodies are of all shapes, sizes, abilities, and hues.
These bodies move through the world
> loving and loved,
> desiring and desired,
> healing and healed.

These bodies hold tightly and tenderly the complexities of being:
attractions,
peeves, passions, scars, successes, traumas, triggers, desires,
rejections, revelry,
heartbreak, intentions, rage, rapture, miscues, magnificence,
contradictions, courage,
determination, discombobulation, dwelling, doubt.

Beautiful and complicated creatures seeking and being sought,
committed and compelled humans navigating the complexities
of the world,
and people loved beyond our imagination by the One who beckons us forth.

By dirt roads and oceans vast, across concrete highways and infinite skies,
by coercion and by consequence, by circumstance, and by
choice—
our journeys converge.

Ancestors and saints,
> generations past,
> generations of today,
> and generations yet to come.
We arrive, we mingle, and we observe.
We step forward, we step back, we pause, we try again.

We engage in a divine dance,
     these bodies, the body,
     all in a space that is God's,
These bodies embody the depth and texture of the Divine,
     seen and unseen,
     known and unknown,
     addressed and avoided.

These bodies are not always in control,
     minds betraying,
     bodies breaking down,
     emotions in disarray,
     mind, body, and spirit,
     swirling, swirling, swirling.

Misfits and strangers uniquely gathered like no place other.
     Gathered by love,
     gathered to love,
     gathered even when we are unable to love,
     and gathered especially when we feel undeserving of
          love.

Woven together in moments momentary and lingering
     to worship God,
     to know what it is to belong,
     to celebrate the jubilance of life,
     to grieve when life is loss,
     to lament and to confess,
     to forgive and to be forgiven,
     to worship, to pray, to march, to nap,
     to argue, to ponder, to weep, to laugh,
     to discern the mind of Christ and the will of God,

to love the other as the world would not want us to love
ourselves,
to affirm and proclaim that we belong to one another,
and in turn we belong to God.

We gather in forms and functions as expansive as creation is
itself,
by affiliation, association, denomination, and affinity,
in living rooms, kitchens, coffee shops, corners,
country churches, town-square sanctuaries, grand
cathedrals,
amid blaring speakers, bright lights, sacred windows,
shiny screens,
pipes floor to ceiling, folding chairs, dripping candles,
well-worn pews, and worn-out carpet,
with cymbals, bells, lyres, guitars, organs, drums,
soundtracks, and turntables.

Basking in the sounds of invitation.
Held in welcomed silence.
God gathers us still.

But these called, sacred, gathered bodies are **HURTING**.

From ancestors and saints past to misfits and strangers of today,
we live in a world that feeds on destruction, rewards hatred, reinforces oppression,
dismisses grief, denies accountability, and manipulates
vulnerability—
and often in the name of God.

We have lost our way.

We have turned and been turned away from God's intentions
and hopes for humanity.
We have brought pain upon my body, your body, our bodies.
Born from anger, disappointment, and mourning,
God weeps with and for me, with and for you, with and for us.
As we desecrate the earth, God weeps.
As we equate light as good and dark as bad, God weeps.
As we pursue profit and perpetuate poverty, God
weeps.
As we criminalize suffering and incarcerate siblings to
invisibility, God weeps.
As we fortify empire and exploit humanity, God weeps.
As we legislate bodies and deny human agency, God
weeps.
As we mock emotions and renounce empathy, God
weeps.
As we choose individualism and abandon the common
good, God weeps.
As we worship "normal" and demonize difference, God
weeps.
As we benefit from unjust systems and justify their
existence, God weeps.
As we deny privilege and default to indifference, God
weeps.
As we choose apathy and forsake the body politic, God
weeps.
As we profit from disparity and blame others for their
desperation, God weeps.

As we deny the sins of our past and reinforce institutions of oppression, God weeps.
And as we embolden violence upon bodies

> who bear darker skin,
> who go unheard,
> who believe differently,
> who love who they love,
> who are deemed weak,
> who are silenced,
> who are unarmed,
> who are not in control,
> who broaden gender,
> who are gifted to our care,
> who are the "enemy,"
> who are different,

God weeps.

We resist and refuse to lament and confess
to that which holds us back from fully knowing God.
Born again and again from anger, disappointment, and mourning, God weeps.
And yet.

And yet we know what it is to be **HEALED**.

To be healed is to be whole.
To move toward healing is to move toward holiness.
In mind. In body. In gut.
In heart. In spirit. In soul.

You cannot be healed if I am still hurting.
I cannot know wholeness if you are still in agony.
We cannot experience either while neighbors and strangers suf-
    fer still.

My wholeness is intricately and intrinsically woven
together with yours and yours with mine.
        Healing is mine is yours is ours.
        Wholeness is ours is yours is mine.

Yet we cannot know healing and wholeness without the One who
    loves us into being.
        God loves healing into the world.
        In whispers. In whimsy. In wonder.
        In exhale. In excitement. In euphoria.
        In solitude. In silence. In subtlety.

Our bodies, minds, and souls are healed by God.
        Healed in ways creative, soothing, beautiful, and bold.
        Healed in ways surprising, subtle, unruly, and old.
        Through boisterous laughter uncontained,
                and anger righteously expressed,
        through sounds that soothe
                and silence that settles,
        though communities organized
                and justice realized,
        through intimacy, generosity, understanding, and rest,
        through equity, jubilance, remembrance, and risk,
        through lament and confession,
        through forgiving and being forgiven,
        through grace offered and grace accepted,

through being seen, being heard, being known.

In all of these things,
in God's good time,
in unexpected ways,
God's healing and wholeness is a mighty balm
for our bone-tired bodies,
for our compassion-fatigued hearts,
and for our weary, weary souls.

I choose to believe in the activity of the Spirit, moved and moving.

The Spirit of God repeatedly sweeps over humanity leaving us **INSPIRED:**
to seek God's hopes for each of us,
to live into God's intentions for the entire body,
and to answer the call to participate in the fulfillment of God's ever-revealing hopes for the world.

The Spirit invites us into relationship and conversations with God.
The Spirit encourages the quest and reveals God in the act of questioning.
The Spirit pokes and prods us to be open and aware that God is with us.
The Spirit revives, refreshes, and reminds us that God will help bear the weight of our weariness.

The Spirit is unwavering in the belief that we have the capacity to know God more.

The Spirit moves around us.
The Spirit moves through us.
The Spirit moves in spite of us.
And when we are open, the Spirit moves us.

The **STORIED** revealing of God's hopes and intentions is intricately woven
in and through our interactions with God—
a delicate conversation between Creator and created.

The Spirit moves through prayer:
Not a checklist but a conversation.
Not performance but release.
Not to control but to relinquish.
Not to manipulate but to listen.
Not with words but also with words.

The Spirit moves through community:
Not to demand but to discern.
Not to fix but to encourage.
Not to confine but to compel.
Not to detach but to engage.
Not to seek perfection but to love perfectly.

The Spirit moves through the Bible:
Not an indifferent collection but an anthology of human
experience.
Not a contract to be enforced but a covenant to be
honored.
Not a map to be followed but an adventure to be
embraced.

Not a literal set of rules but evolving truths to be revealed.

Not a weapon of faith but a wellspring of liberation.

The Spirit moves in the in-between:

Not always knowing where but trusting God is present.

Not always knowing how but trusting God is active.

Not always knowing when but trusting God is near.

Not always knowing why but trusting God is faithful.

Not always knowing but trusting that God is.

Through these windows

we meet ourselves,

we meet others,

our understanding of God is expanded,

the movements of God are made real,

and the revealed and revealing story of God is made known.

It is into the revealing story of God that we are **COMPELLED** to go.

Where we are called to serve God and others.

Where we are drawn into a deeper relationship with God.

Where we are thrust into the struggles of the world.

It is in God's revealing story where we grow into who God intends us to become.

Not if we go, but as we go.

As we go, we seek:

Wisdom. Healing. Growth. Love.
As we go, we are healed:
>   By others. By ourselves. By surprise. By love.
As we go, we offer back to God:
>   Our talents. Our resources. Our humanity. Our love.
As we go, we share what and who we know God to be.
>   Hope. Joy. Peace. Love.

As it has been with generations before and will be for generations to come,
God's story has and will be **REVEALED** to God's gathered people.

The story will meander,
>   but God's time is God's time.
The story will confuse,
>   but God will guide us if we choose to follow.
The story will contradict,
>   but God's perfection lies in a willingness to change.
The story will be deemed weak,
>   but God reimagines what is powerful.
The story will seem like a distant figure emerging from the mist-worn fog,
>   but when we see God, we really see God.
And we will know.
The story will be revealed.

I choose to believe in grace made real through Jesus Christ.

For the complete and complex humanity of Jesus,
and the mysterious and boundless divinity of the Christ,

I am **GRATEFUL**.

Grateful for the prophet, activist, and agitator,
>   who speaks God's hopes, intentions, and truth into the
>   world.

Grateful for the pastor, protector, and gatherer,
>   who curates space for curiosity, compassion, and
>   kinship.

Grateful for the priest, steward, and guide,
>   who tends, grounds, and guides the spirits of those on
>   the journey.

Grateful for the poet, artist, and creative,
>   who instigates, inspires, and invites exploration of divine
>   possibility.

Grateful for the unpretentious life of Christ,
>   the teacher and friend.

Grateful for the revelatory death of Christ,
>   the offender and threat.

And grateful for the promised resurrection of Christ,
>   the seeker and solace.

For in the life, death, and resurrection of the one called Christ,
>   we are reconnected to God,
>   reunited with the saints,
>   loved for eternity,
>   and promised that one day there will be a new heaven
>   and new earth.

For this I am grateful.
For this we are grateful.

In all of this, we find mystery, meaning, and motivation.

I believe in the **GENEROUS** spirit of God.

God has been generous to me, so I give back to God
    all that I have the courage and faith to offer.
When the fear of scarcity causes me to forsake abundance,
    I choose generosity.
When the insidiousness of convenience causes me to avoid
discomfort,
    I choose generosity.
When capitalism makes me want to commodify what I offer,
    I choose generosity.
When arrogance causes me to tie strings to my gifts,
    I choose generosity.
When despair causes me to ask, "Why bother?"
    I choose generosity.
When I forget that I have chosen to believe that, in life and in
death, I belong to God,
    I choose generosity.

I choose generosity because God has been generous to me.

With a posture of plenty, wisdom, and faith I offer back to God.
    What I have is not mine to store up and hoard.
    What I do is not meant for acknowledgment and
    affirmation.
    What I believe is not meant to remain stagnant and
    stale.

What I have, what I do, what I believe come from God,

with a spirit of hopeful joy,
with a posture of abundant generosity,
with trust in God that the world would deny.

I return all that I am and all that I have to God.
Time. Talent. Treasure.
Energy. Expertise. Wealth.
Presence. Passion. Privilege.

I choose generosity because God has been generous to me.

As we go, we join with other seeking and searching souls,
we name, we seal, and we proclaim our commitment to
the faith.

We claim the faith that we chose to believe
in ritual and rite,
sacred and sacramental,
proclaimed and public,
jubilant and free.

In baptism we are **RENEWED**.
Renewed, refreshed, and reminded by the water of life,
the flowing waters of our ancestors,
the living water of future generations.
Baptized not as a transactional act that purchases God's favor,
but as a response to what God is doing in our lives and
the world.
Baptized not to settle for a future bound by scarcity,
but to see dreams realized that are fueled by the abundance of God.

Baptized not as a private gesture to prove our purity of faith,
> but as a public act to proclaim our devotion to one
> another.

Baptized not as a final destination on our journey to know God,
> but as a commitment to return over and over again to
> the place

where the waterfalls, rivers, and streams of living water flow
> unrestrained.

At the communion table, we are **FED**.
> A table with space for stranger, sibling, sinner, and saint,
> a table set with intention, tenderness, and care,
> a table filled with an overflowing feast of love.

An ever-expanding table for all who wish to take their place.

Here our hunger is nourished by the bread of life,
> the bread blessed and broken.

Here our thirst is quenched by the cup of the new promise,
> the cup poured and passed.

Here a feast of faith is joyfully shared by the people of God,
> a feast that nourishes and nurtures us all for the journey
> home.

As we are sent, as we are called, as we choose to go into the
> world,
> the body of Christ,
> dwelling amid the body politic,
> seeking the common good for all.

We go with minds and hearts that are **HUMBLE**
> to share a faith strengthened by always seeking God.

We go with hands and feet that are **JUST**
>to take part in God's healing of a hurting world.

We go with souls and spirits that are **KIND**
>to tell God's story of dignity, empathy, and love.

And we go **LED** by the God who sends us, calls us back, and sends us again
>to be and become more than we could ever dream for ourselves.

All these things I choose to believe.
>—AMEN.

Creating Your Faith Montage

So now it's your turn! When you are ready, consider creating your own faith montage. Engaging in this exercise helps to give form to your faith and acts as a living, sweeping, audacious account of what you believe. Your montage will not answer every question with finitude; the power is found in the curiosity, inquiry, courage, phrasing, imagery, and cadence. The feel and flow must be yours, a space of inspiration that you can return to in order to remind you of where you have been and prompt you toward where you are headed next. Your faith montage will be a living, breathing, evolving story of faith, yours and yours alone.

Materials Needed

- Blocked-out time to sink into a process of inquiry and exploration
- Space that offers a creative and focused atmosphere
- Journal, notepad, canvas, or other medium
- Pens, paint, or other ways to record your ideas

Guidance and Suggested Process

- Sit with what you have read: journal some words, pray some prayers, or take long walks. Take some time to see what bubbles up in your soul.

- Reflect on the questions at the end of each chapter. In addition to the questions, think about what was missing, what struck you. Take note of your responses to the prompts that begin with, "What are three beliefs . . .?"
- If you need a prompt, begin with a light structure below. I hope and expect that you will divert from this as the spirit guides demand, but hopefully a place to begin will be helpful to get you started.
- As you think about creating your faith montage, open yourself up to different words, differing media, colors, textures, etc.

Structure Prompts

About God, I choose to believe . . .

About the Spirit, I choose to believe . . .

About Jesus, I choose to believe . . .

About the church, I choose to believe . . .

About the Bible, I choose to believe . . .

About baptism, I choose to believe . . .

About communion, I choose to believe . . .

About prayer, I choose to believe . . .

About politics, I choose to believe . . .

About _____, I choose to believe . . .

About _____, I choose to believe . . .

About _____, I choose to believe . . .

If you create your own faith montage, I would love to see a copy. Again, you can find me at @breyeschow on all the social platforms.

Acknowledgments

*P*eople. The people and communities who have helped to shape and form my theological perspectives and political personality are too numerous to name. From church sanctuary to soccer sideline to school communities, I am grateful for all of those who have poured their wisdom, courage, challenge, and comfort into my particular journey of faith and relationship to God.

Places. For all of the places where I found myself writing, editing, and planting my face on the tabletop when the words would not come: First and foremost for this book, Spectra Coffee in San Jose, where the staff are lovely, the coffee tasty, and the culinary magicians in the kitchen conjure up *the* best avocado toast ever; Happy Girl Kitchen in Pacific Grove, where, again, the avocado toast is scrumptious and they make the best bread; Captain Stokers in Monterey, where the avocado bowl has been mastered (yes, I know, I have an avocado problem); Java Café in Maui, where I spent many early morning vacation hours writing, fueled by iced coffee, smoked salmon bagels, and time away from those pesky "tourists"; Pioneer Café in the Yucca Valley, where the lox bagel is amazing; multiple Starbucks, where I get my "iced chocolate almond milk shaken espresso with an extra shot of malt" comfort beverage; Philz Coffee in general, with a special shoutout to the Middlefield location in Palo Alto; Obet & Del's in Los Angeles, where the Filipino iced coffee is masarap; and all of the other random cafés, coffee shops, and tea houses around the country where I may have parked for an hour or six. These "third spaces" in society are a balm to the wounds of worldly division, and I am grateful for all of those who fill this vital role.

Pups. And yes, as always, my puppers, Vespa the English Bull Terrier and Bernie the Beagador. While Bernie shows his love through his consistent grumpy old man vibes, Vespa helped to nurse me through my Covid recovery and subsequent long Covid terribleness. She was always willing to stare at my incessant and annoying Instagram reel-making in exchange for a good snuggle on the couch or a bully stick. I'm not sure how many more books Vespa will help to write, but it's safe to say that pup has been a balm to my spirit and soul.

Valerie: the depth of gratitude that I have for my editor is immeasurable. She championed this project from the beginning, quickly grasped my voice and intentions, pushed and prodded me with compassion, eased my tender author anxieties more than once, and helped to bring clarity to this book beyond what I could have imagined. Thank you, Valerie!

Lastly, much love to my spouse, Robin, and my three children, Annie, Abby, and Ev, for their patience, support, and love.